BÉBÉE,

OR

TWO LITTLE WOODEN SHOES.

BÉBÉE,

OR

TWO LITTLE WOODEN SHOES.

A STORY.

BY "OUIDA,"

AUTHOR OF "STRATHMORE," "TRICOTRIN," "UNDER TWO FLAGS," "IDALIA," "PASCAREL," ETC.

PHILADELPHIA:

J. B. LIPPINCOTT & CO.

1874.

TWO LITTLE WOODEN SHOES.

CHAPTER I.

BEBEE sprang out of bed at daybreak. She was sixteen.

It seemed a very wonderful thing to be as much as that—sixteen—a woman quite.

A cock was crowing under her lattice—he said how old you are!—how old you are!—every time that he sounded his clarion.

She opened the lattice and wished him good-day, with a laugh. It was so pleasant to be woke by him and to think that no one in all the world could ever call one a child any more.

There was a kid bleating in the shed. There was a thrush singing in the dusk of the sycamore-leaves. There was a calf lowing to its mother away there beyond the fence. There were dreamy muffled bells ringing in the distance from many steeples and belfries where the city was; they all said one thing: "How good it is to be so old as that—how good, how very good!"

Bébée was very pretty.

No one in all Brabant ever denied that. To look at her it seemed as if she had so lived among the flowers that she had grown like them, and only looked a bigger blossom—that was all.

She wore two little wooden shoes and a little cotton cap, and a gray kirtle—linen in summer, serge in winter; but the little feet in the shoes were like rose-leaves, and the cap was as white as a lily, and the gray kirtle was like the bark of the bough that the apple-blossom parts, and peeps out of, to blush in the sun.

The flowers had been the only godmothers that she had ever had, and fairy godmothers too.

The marigolds and the sunflowers had given her their ripe, rich gold to tint her hair; the lupins and irises had lent their azure to her eyes; the moss-rose buds had made her pretty mouth; the arum lilies had uncurled their softness for her skin; and the lime-blossoms had given her their frank, fresh, innocent fragrance.

The winds had blown, and the rains had rained, and the sun had shone on her, indeed, and had warmed the whiteness of her limbs, but they had only given to her body and her soul a hardy, breeze-blown freshness like that of a field cowslip.

She had never been called anything but Bébée.

One summer day Antoine Mäes—a French subject, but a Belgian by adoption and habit, an old man who got his meagre living by tilling the garden-plot about his hut and selling flowers in the city squares—Antoine, going into Brussels for his day's trade, had seen a gray bundle floating among the water-lilies in the bit of water near his hut and had hooked it out to land, and found a year-old child in it, left to drown, no doubt, but saved by the lilies, and laughing gleefully at fate.

Some lace-worker, blind with the pain of toil, or some peasant woman harder of heart than the oxen in her yoke, had left it there to drift away to death, not reckoning for the inward ripple of the current or the toughness of the lily-leaves and stems.

Old Antoine took it to his wife, and the wife, a childless and aged soul, begged leave to keep it; and the two poor lonely, simple folks grew to care for the homeless, motherless thing, and they and the people about all called it Bébée—only Bébée.

The church got at it and added to it a saint's name; but for all its little world it remained Bébée—Bébée when it trotted no higher than the red carnation-heads;—Bébée when its yellow curls touched as high as the lavender-bush;—Bébée on this proud day when the thrush's song and the cock's crow found her sixteen years old.

Old Antoine's hut stood in a little patch of garden ground with a brier hedge all round it, in that byway which lies between Laeken and Brussels, in the heart of flat, green Brabant, where there are beautiful meadows and tall, flowering hedges, and forest-trees, and fern-filled ditches, and a little piece of water, deep and cool, where the swans sail all day long, and the silvery willows dip and sway with the wind.

Turn aside from the highway, and there it lies to-day, and all the place brims over with grass, and boughs, and blossoms, and flowering beans, and wild dog-roses; and there are a few cottages and cabins there near the pretty water, and farther there is an old church, sacred to St. Guido; and beyond go the green level country and the endless wheat-fields, and the old mills with their red sails against the sun; and beyond all these the pale blue, sea-like horizon of the plains of Flanders.

It was a pretty little hut, pink all over like a sea-shell, in the fashion that the Netherlanders love; and its two little square lattices were dark with creeping plants and big rose-bushes, and its roof, so low that you could touch it, was golden and green with all the lichens and stoneworts that are known on earth.

Here Bébée grew from year to year; and soon learned to be big enough and hardy enough to tie up bunches of stocks and pinks for the market, and then to carry a basket for herself, trotting by Antoine's side along the green roadway and into the white, wide streets; and in the market the buyers—most often of all when they were young mothers—would seek out the little golden head and the beautiful frank blue eyes, and buy Bébée's lilies and carnations whether they wanted them or not. So that old Mäes used to cross himself and say that, thanks to Our Lady, trade was thrice as stirring since the little one had stretched out her rosy fingers with the flowers.

All the same, however stirring trade might be in summer, when the long winters came and the Montagne de la Cour was a sharp slope of ice, and the pinnacles of St. Gudule were all frosted white with snow, and the hot-house flowers alone could fill the market, and the country gardens were bitter black wind-swept desolations where the chilly roots huddled themselves together underground like homeless children in a cellar,—then the money gained in the time of leaf and blossom was all needed to buy a black loaf and fagot of wood; and many a day in the little pink hut Bébée rolled herself up in her bed like a dormouse, to forget in sleep that she was supperless and as cold as a frozen robin.

So that when Antoine Mäes grew sick and died, more from age and weakness than any real disease, there were only a few silver crowns in the brown jug hidden in the thatch; and the hut itself, with its patch of ground, was all that he could leave to Bébée.

"Live in it, little one, and take nobody in it to worry you, and be good to the bird and the goat, and be sure to keep the flowers blowing," said the old man with his last breath; and sobbing her heart out by his bedside, Bébée vowed to do his bidding.

She was not quite fourteen then, and when she

had laid her old friend to rest in the rough green graveyard about St. Guido, she was very sorrowful and lonely—poor little, bright Bébée, who had never hardly known a worse woe than to run the thorns of the roses into her fingers, or to cry because a thrush was found starved to death in the snow.

Bébée went home, and sat down in a corner and thought.

The hut was her own, and her own the little green triangle just then crowded with its Mayday blossom in all the colors of the rainbow. She was to live in it, and never let the flowers die—so he had said; good, rough old ugly Antoine Mäes, who had been to her as father, mother, country, king, and law.

The sun was shining.

Through the little square of the lattice she could see the great tulips opening in the grass and a bough of the apple-tree swaying in the wind. A chaffinch clung to the bough, and swung to and fro singing. The door stood open, with the broad, bright day beaming through; and Bébée's little world came streaming in with it—the world which dwelt in the half-dozen cottages that fringed this green lane of hers like beavers'-nests pushed out under the leaves on to the water's edge.

They came in, six or eight of them, all women; trim, clean, plain Brabant peasants, hard working, kindly of nature, and shrewd in their own simple matters; people who labored in the fields all the day long, or worked themselves blind over the lace pillows in the city.

"You are too young to live alone, Bébée," said the first of them. "My old mother shall come and keep house for you."

"Nay—better come and live with me, Bébée," said the second. "I will give you bit and drop, and clothing, too, for the right to your plot of ground."

"That is to cheat her," said the third. "Hark here, Bébée: my sister, who is a lone woman, as you know well, shall come and bide with you, and ask you nothing—nothing at all—only you shall just give her a crust, perhaps, and a few flowers to sell sometimes."

"No, no," said the fourth; "that will not do. You let me have the garden and the hut, Bébée, and my sons shall till the place for you; and I will live with you myself, and leave the boys the cabin—so you will have all the gain, do you not see, dear little one?"

"Pooh!" said the fifth, stouter and better clothed than the rest. "You are all eager for your own good, not for hers. Now I—Father Francis says we should all do as we would be done by—I will take Bébée to live with me, all for nothing; and we will root the flowers up and plant it with good cabbages and potatoes and salad plants. And I will stable my cows in the hut to sweeten it after a dead man, and I will take my chance of making money out of it, and no one can speak more fair than that when one sees what weather is, and thinks what insects do; and all the year round, winter and summer, Bébée here will want for nothing, and have to take no care for herself whatever."

She who spoke, Mère Krebs, was the best-to-do woman in the little lane, having two cows of her own and ear-rings of solid silver, and a green cart, and a big dog that took the milk into Brussels. She was heard, therefore, with respect, and a short silence followed her words.

But it was very short; and a hubbub of voices crossed each other after it as the speakers grew hotter against one another and more eager to convince each other of the disinterestedness and delicacy of their offers of aid.

Through it all Bébée sat quite quiet on the edge of the little truckle-bed, with her eyes fixed on the apple-bough and the singing chaffinch.

She heard them all patiently.

They were all her good friends, friends old and true. This one had given her cherries a score of summers. That other had bought her a little waxen Jesus at the Kermesse. The old woman in the blue linen skirt had taken her to her first communion. She who wanted her sister to have the crust and the flowers, had brought her a beautiful painted book of hours that had cost a whole franc. Another had given her the solitary wonder, travel, and foreign feast of her whole life—a day fifteen miles away at the fair at Mechlin. The last speaker of all had danced her on her knee a hundred times in babyhood, and told her legends, and let her ride in the green cart behind big curly-coated Tambour.

Bébée did not doubt that these trusty old friends meant well by her, and yet a certain heavy sense fell on her that in all these counsels there was not the same whole-hearted and frank goodness that had prompted the gifts to her of the waxen Jesus, and the Kermesse of Mechlin.

Bébée did not reason, because she was too little a thing and too trustful; but she felt, in a vague, sorrowful fashion, that they were all of them trying to make some benefit out of her poor little heritage, with small regard for herself at the root of their speculations.

Bébée was a child; wholly a child; body and soul were both as fresh in her as a golden crocus just born out of the snows. But she was not a little fool, though people sometimes called her so because she would sit in the moments of her leisure with her blue eyes on the far-away clouds like a thing in a dream.

She heard them patiently till the cackle of shrill voices had exhausted itself, and the six women stood on the sunny mud floor of the hut eyeing each other with venomous glances; for though they were good neighbors at all times, each, in this matter, was hungry for the advantages to be got out of old Antoine's plot of ground. They were very poor; they toiled in the scorched or frozen fields all weathers, or spent from dawn to nightfall pouring over their cobweb lace; and to save a sou or gain a cabbage was of moment to them only second to the keeping of their souls secure of heaven by Lenten mass and Easter psalm.

Bébée listened to them all, and the tears dried on her cheeks, and her pretty rosebud lips curled close in one another.

"You are very good, no doubt, all of you," she said at last. "But I cannot tell you that I am thankful, for my heart is like a stone, and I think it is not so very much for me as it is for the hut that you are speaking. Perhaps it is wrong in me to say so—yes, I am wrong, I am sure,—you are all kind, and I am only Bébée. But you see he told me to live here and take care of the flowers, and I must do it, that is certain. I will ask Father Francis, if you wish; but if he tells me I am wrong, as you do, I shall stay here all the same."

And in answer to their expostulations and condemnation, she only said the same thing over again always, in different words, but to the same steadfast purpose. The women clamored about her for an hour in reproach and rebuke; she was a baby indeed, she was a little fool, she was a naughty, obstinate child, she was an ungrateful willful little creature, who ought to be beaten till she was blue, if only there was anybody that had the right to do it!

"But there is nobody that has the right," said Bébée, getting angry and standing upright on the floor, with Antoine's old gray cat in her round arms. "He told me to stay here, and he would not have said so if it had been wrong; and I am old enough to do for myself, and I am not afraid, and who is there that would hurt me? Oh, yes; go and tell Father Francis, if you like. I do not believe he will blame me, but if he do, I must bear it. Even if he shut the church door on me, I will obey Antoine, and the flowers will know I am right, and they will let no evil spirits touch me, for the flowers are strong for that; they talk to the angels in the night."

What use was it to argue with a little idiot like this? Indeed, peasants never do argue; they use abuse.

It is their only form of logic.

They used it to Bébée, rating her soundly, as became people who were old enough to be her grandmothers, and who knew that she had been raked out of their own pond, and had no more real place in creation than a water-rat, as one might say.

The women were kindly, and had never thrown this truth against her before, and in fact, to be a foundling was no sort of disgrace to their sight; but anger is like wine, and makes the depths of the mind shine clear, and all the mud that is in the depths stink in the light; and in their wrath at not sharing Antoine's legacy, the good souls said bitter things that in calm moments they would no more have uttered than they would have taken up a knife to slit her throat.

They talked themselves hoarse with impatience and chagrin, and went backwards over the threshold, their wooden shoes and their shrill voices keeping a clattering chorus. By this time it was evening; the sun had gone off the floor, and the bird had done singing.

Bébée stood in the same place, hardening her little heart, whilst big and bitter tears swelled into her eyes, and fell on the soft fur of the sleeping cat.

She only very vaguely understood why it was in any sense shameful to have been raked out of the water-lilies like a drowning field-mouse, as they had said it was.

She and Antoine had often talked of that summer morning when he had found her there among the leaves, and Bébée and he had laughed over it gayly, and she had been quite proud in her innocent fashion that she had had a fairy and the flowers for her mother and godmothers, which Antoine always told her was the case beyond any manner of doubt. Even Father Francis, hearing the pretty harmless fiction, had never deemed it his duty to disturb her pleasure in it, being a good, cheerful old man, who thought that woe and wisdom both come soon enough to bow young shoulders and to silver young curls without his interference.

Bébée had always thought it quite a fine thing to have been born of water-lilies, with the sun for her father, and when people in Brussels had asked her of her parentage, seeing her stand in the market with a certain look on her that was not like other children, had always gravely answered in the purest good faith,—

"My mother was a flower."

"You are a flower, at any rate," they would say in return; and Bébée had been always quite content.

But now she was doubtful; she was rather perplexed than sorrowful.

These good friends of hers seemed to see some new sin about her. Perhaps, after all, thought Bébée, it might have been better to have had a human mother who would have taken care of her now that old Antoine was dead, instead of those beautiful, gleaming, cold water-lilies which went to sleep on their green velvet beds, and did not certainly care when the thorns ran into her fingers, or the pebbles got in her wooden shoes.

In some vague way, disgrace and envy—the twin Discords of the world—touched her innocent cheek with their hot breath, and as the evening fell, Bébée felt very lonely and a little wistful.

She had been always used to run out in the pleasant twilight-time among the flowers and water them, Antoine filling the can from the well; and the neighbors would come and lean against the little low wall, knitting and gossiping; and the big dogs, released from harness, would poke their heads through the wicket for a crust; and the children would dance and play Colin Maillard on the green by the water, and she, when the flowers were no longer thirsted, would join them, and romp and dance and sing the gayest of them all.

But now the buckets hung at the bottom of the

well, and the flowers hungered in vain, and the neighbors held aloof, and she shut-to the hut door and listened to the rain which began to fall, and cried herself to sleep all alone in her tiny kingdom.

When the dawn came the sun rose red and warm; the grass and boughs sparkled; a lark sang; Bébée awoke sad in heart, indeed, for her lost old friend, but brighter and braver.

"Each of them wants to get something out of me," thought the child. "Well, I will live alone, then, and do my duty, just as he said. The flowers will never let any real harm come, though they do look so indifferent and smiling sometimes, and though not one of them hung their heads when his coffin was carried through them yesterday."

That want of sympathy in the flowers troubled her.

The old man had loved them so well; and they had all looked as glad as ever, and had laughed saucily in the sun, and not even a rosebud turned the paler as the poor still stiffened limbs went by in the wooden shell.

"I suppose God cares—but I wish they did," said Bébée, to whom the garden was more intelligible than Providence.

"Why do you not care?" she asked the pinks, shaking the rain-drops off their curled rosy petals.

The pinks leaned lazily against their sticks, and seemed to say, "Why should we care for anything, unless a slug be eating us?—*that* is real woe, if you like."

Bébée, without her sabots on, wandered thoughtfully among the sweet wet sunlightened labyrinths of blossom, her pretty bare feet treading the narrow grassy paths with pleasure in their coolness.

"He was so good to you," she said reproachfully to the great gaudy gillyflowers and the painted sweet-peas. "He never let you know heat or cold—he never let the worm gnaw or the snail harm you;—he would get up in the dark to see after your wants,—and when the ice froze over you, he was there to loosen your chains. Why do you not care, any one of you?"

"How silly you are!" said the flowers. "You must be a butterfly or a poet, Bébée, to be as foolish as that. Some one will do all he did. We are of market value, you know. Care, indeed!—when the sun is so warm, and there is not an earwig in the place to trouble us."

The flowers were not always so selfish as this; and perhaps the sorrow in Bébée's heart made their callousness seem harder than it really was.

When we suffer very much ourselves, anything that smiles in the sun seems cruel—a child, a bird, a dragon-fly—nay, even a fluttering ribbon, or a spear-grass that waves in the wind.

There was a little shrine at the corner of the garden, set into the wall; a niche with a bit of glass and a picture of the Virgin, so battered that no one could trace any feature of it.

It had been there for centuries, and was held in

great veneration; and old Antoine had always cut the choicest buds of his roses and sèt them in a delf pot in front of it every other morning all the summer long. Bébée, whose religion was the sweetest, vaguest mingling of Pagan and Christian myths, and whose faith in fairies and in saints was exactly equal in strength and in ignorance—Bébée filled the delf pot anew carefully, then knelt down on the turf in that little green corner, and prayed in devout hopeful childish good faith to the awful unknown Powers who were to her only as gentle guides and kindly playmates.

Was she too familiar with the Holy Mother?

She was almost fearful that she was; but then the Holy Mother loved flowers so well, Bébée would not feel aloof from her, nor be afraid.

"When one cuts the best blossoms for her, and tries to be good, and never tells a lie," thought Bébée, "I am quite sure, as she loves the lilies, that she will never altogether forget me."

So she said to the Mother of Christ fearlessly, and nothing doubting; and then rose for her daily work of cutting the flowers for the market in Brussels.

By the time her baskets were full, her fowls fed, her goat foddered, her starling's cage cleaned, her hut door locked, and her wooden shoes clattering on the sunny road into the city, Bébée was almost content again, though ever and again, as she trod the familiar ways, the tears dimmed her eyes as she remembered that old Antoine would never again hobble over the stones beside her.

"You are a little willful one, and too young to live alone," said Father Francis, meeting her in the lane.

But he did not scold her seriously; and she kept to her resolve; and the women, who were good at heart, took her back into favor again; and so Bébée had her own way, and the fairies, or the saints, or both together, took care of her; and so it came to pass that all alone she heard the cock crow whilst it was dark, and woke to the grand and amazing truth that this warm, fragrant, dusky June morning found her full sixteen years old.

CHAPTER II.

THE two years had not been all playtime, any more than they had been all summer. When one has not father, or mother, or brother, and all one's friends have barely bread enough for themselves, life cannot be very easy, nor its crusts very many at any time.

Bébée had a cherub's mouth, and a dreamer's eyes, and a poet's thoughts sometimes in her own untaught and unconscious fashion.

But all the same she was a little hard-working Brabant peasant girl; up whilst the birds twittered in the dark; to bed when the red sun sank beyond the far blue line of the plains; she hoed, and dug, and watered, and planted her little plot; she kept her cabin as clean as a fresh-blossomed primrose; she milked her goat, and swept her floor; she sat, all the warm days, in the town, selling her flowers, and in the winter-time, when her garden yielded her nothing, she strained her sight over lace-making in the city to get the small bit of food that stood between her and that hunger which to the poor means death.

A hard life: very hard when hail and snow made

the streets of Brussels like slopes of ice; a little hard even in the gay summer-time when she sat under the awning fronting the Maison du Roi; but all the time the child throve on it, and was happy, and dreamed of many graceful and gracious things whilst she was weeding among her lilies, or tracing the threads to and fro on her lace pillow.

Now—when she woke to the full sense of her wonderful sixteen years—Bébée, standing barefoot on the mud-floor, was as pretty a sight as was to be seen betwixt Scheldt and Rhine.

The sun had only left a soft warmth like an apricot's on her white skin. Her limbs, though strong as a mountain pony's, were slender and well shaped. Her hair curled in shiny crumpled masses, and tumbled about her shoulders. Her pretty round plump little breast was white as the lilies in the grass without, and in this blooming time of her little life Bébée, in her way, was beautiful as a peach-bloom is beautiful, and her innocent, courageous, happy eyes had dreams in them underneath their laughter—dreams that went farther than the green woods of Laeken, farther even than the white clouds of summer.

She could not move among them idly as poets and girls love to do; she had to be active amidst them, else drought and rain, and worm and snail, and blight and frost would have made havoc of their fairest hopes.

The loveliest love is that which dreams high above all storms, unsoiled by all burdens; but perhaps the strongest love is that which, whilst it adores, drags its feet through mire, and burns its brow in heat, for the thing beloved.

So Bébée dreamed in her garden ; but all the time for sake of it hoed and dug, and hurt her hands, and tired her limbs, and bowed her shoulders under the great metal pails from the well.

This wondrous morning, with the bright burden of her sixteen years upon her, she dressed herself quickly and fed her fowls, and, happy as a bird, went to sit on her little wooden stool in the doorway.

There had been fresh rain in the night: the garden was radiant; the smell of the wet earth was sweeter than all perfumes that are burned in palaces.

The dripping rosebuds nodded against her hair as she went out; the starling called to her—"Bébée, Bébée—bonjour, bonjour." These were all the words it knew. It said the same words a thousand times a week. But to Bébée it seemed that the starling most certainly knew that she was sixteen years old that day.

Breaking her bread into the milk, she sat in the dawn and thought, without knowing that she thought it, "How good it is to live when one is young!"

Old people say the same thing often, but they sigh when they say it. Bébée smiled.

Mère Krebs opened her door in the next cottage, and nodded over the wall.

"What a fine thing to be sixteen!—a merry year, Bébée."

Marthe, the carpenter's wife, came out from her gate, broom in hand.

"The Holy Saints keep you, Bébée; why, you are quite a woman now!"

The little children of Varnhart, the charcoal-burner, who were as poor as any mouse in the old churches, rushed out of their little home up the lane, bringing with them a cake stuck full of sugar and seeds, and tied round with a blue ribbon, that their mother had made that very week, all in her honor.

"Only see, Bébée! Such a grand cake!" they shouted, dancing down the lane. "Jules picked the plums, and Jeanne washed the almonds, and Christine took the ribbon off her own communion cap—all for you—all for you; but you will let us come and eat it too?"

Old gran'mère Bishot, who was the oldest woman about Laeken, hobbled through the grass on her crutches and nodded her white shaking head, and smiled at Bébée.

"I have nothing to give you, little one—except my blessing, if you care for that."

Bébée ran out, breaking from the children, and knelt down in the wet grass, and bent her pretty sunny head to the benediction.

Trine, the miller's wife, the richest woman of them all, called to the child from the steps of the mill,—

"A merry year, and the blessing of Heaven, Bébée! Come up, and here is my first dish of cherries for you; not tasted one myself; they will make you a feast with Varnhart's cake, though she should have known better, so poor as she is. Charity begins at home, and these children's stomachs are empty."

Bébée ran up and then down again gleefully, with her lapful of big black cherries; Tambour, the old white dog, who had used to drag her about in his milk-cart, leaping on her in sympathy and congratulation.

"What a supper we will have!" she cried to the charcoal-burner's children, who were turning summersaults in the dock-leaves, while the swans stared and hissed.

When one is sixteen, cherries and a cake have a flavor of Paradise still, especially when they are tasted twice, or thrice at most, in all the year.

An old man called to her as she went by his door. All these little cabins lie close together, with only their apple-trees, or their tall beans, or their hedges of thorn between them; you may ride by and never notice them if you do not look for them under the leaves closely, as you would for thrushes'-nests.

He, too, was very old; a life-long neighbor and gossip of Antoine's; he had been a day-laborer in these same fields all his years, and had never traveled farther than where the red mill-sails turned among the colza and the corn.

"Come in, my pretty one, for a second," he whispered, with an air of mystery that made Bébée's heart quicken with expectancy. "Come in; I have something for you. They were my dead daughter's—you have heard me talk of her —Lisette, who died forty year or more ago, they say; for me I think it was yesterday. Mère Krebs —she is a hard woman—heard me talking of my girl. She burst out laughing, 'Lord's sake, fool, why, your girl would be sixty now an she had lived.' Well, so it may be; you see, the new mill was put up the week she died, and you call the new mill old; but, my girl, she is young to me. Always young. Come here, Bébée."

Bébée went after him, a little awed, into the dusky interior, that smelt of stored apples and of dried herbs that hung from the roof. There was a walnut-wood press, such as the peasants of France and the low countries keep their home-spun linen in and their old lace that serves for the nuptials and baptisms of half a score of generations.

The old man unlocked it with a trembling hand, and there came from it an odor of dead lavender and of withered rose-leaves.

On the shelves there were a girl's set of clothes, and a girl's sabots, and a girl's communion veil and wreath.

"They are all hers," he whispered; "all hers. And sometimes in the evening-time I see her coming along the lane for them—do you not know?

There is nothing changed; nothing changed; the grass, and the trees, and the huts, and the pond are all here—why should she only be gone away?"

"Antoine is gone."

"Yes. But he was old; my girl is young."

He stood a moment, with the press door open, a perplexed trouble in his dim eyes; the divine faith of love and the mule-like stupidity of ignorance made him cling to this one thought without power of judgment in it.

"They say she would be sixty," he said, with a little dreary smile. "But that is absurd, you know. Why, she had cheeks like yours, and she would run—no lapwing could fly faster over corn. These are her things, you see; yes—all of them. That is the sprig of sweetbrier she wore in her belt the day before the wagon knocked her down and killed her. I have never touched the things. But look here, Bébée, you are a good child and true, and like her just a little. I mean to give you her silver clasps. They were her great-great-great-grandmother's before her. God knows how old they are not. And a girl should have some little wealth of that sort—and for Antoine's sake——"

The old man stayed behind, closing the press door upon the lavender-scented clothes, and sitting down in the dull shadow of the hut to think of his daughter, dead forty summers and more.

Bébée went out with the brave broad silver

clasps about her waist, and the tears wet on her cheeks for a grief not her own.

To be killed just when one was young, and was loved like that, and all the world was in its May-day flower! The silver felt cold to her touch—as cold as though it were the dead girl's hands that held her.

The garlands that the children strung of daisies and hung about her had never chilled her so.

But little Jeanne, the youngest of the charcoal-burner's little tribe, running to meet her, screamed with glee, and danced in the gay morning.

"Oh, Bébée! how you glitter! Did the Virgin send you that off her own altar? Let me see—let me touch! Is it made of the stars or of the sun?"

And Bébée danced with the child, and the silver gleamed and sparkled, and all the people came running out to see, and the milk-carts were half an hour later for town, and the hens cackled loud unfed, and the men even stopped on their way to the fields and paused, with their scythes on their shoulders, to stare at the splendid gift.

"There is not such another set of clasps in Brabant; old work you could make a fortune of in the curiosity-shops in the Montagne," said Trine Krebs, going up the steps of her mill-house. "But, all the same, you know, Bébée, things cff a dead body bring mischance sometimes."

But Bébée danced with the child, and did not hear.

Whose fête day had ever begun like this one of hers?

She was a little poet at heart, and should not have cared for such vanities; but when one is only sixteen, and has only a little rough woolen frock, and sits in the market-place or the lace-room, with other girls around, how should one be altogether indifferent to a broad, embossed, beautiful shield of silver that sparkled with each step one took?

A quarter of an hour idle thus was all, however, that Bébée or her friends could spare at five o'clock on a summer morning, when the city was waiting for its eggs, its honey, its flowers, its cream, and its butter, and Tambour was shaking his leather harness in impatience to be off with his milk-cans.

So Bébée, all holiday though it was, and heroine though she felt herself, ran in-doors, put up her cakes and cherries, cut her two basketfuls out of the garden, locked her hut, and went on her quick and happy little feet along the grassy paths toward the city.

The sorting and tying up of the flowers she always left until she was sitting under the awning in front of the Broodhuis; the same awning, tawny as an autumn pear and weather-blown as an old sail, which had served to shelter Antoine Mäes from heat and rain through all the years of his life.

"Go to the Madeleine; you will make money there, with your pretty blue eyes, Bébée," people had said to her of late; but Bébée had shaken her head.

Where she had sat in her babyhood at Antoine's feet, she would sit so long as she sold flowers in Brussels—here, underneath the shadow of the Gothic towers that saw Egmont die.

Old Antoine had never gone into the grand market that is fashioned after the Madeleine of Paris, and where in the cool, wet, sweet-smelling halls, all the flowers of Brabant are spread in bouquets fit for the bridal of Una, and large as the shield of the Red-Cross Knight.

Antoine could not compete with all those treasures of greenhouse and stove. He had always had his little stall among those which spread their tawny awnings and their merry hardy blossoms under the shadow of the Hôtel de Ville, in the midst of the buyings and sellings, the games and the quarrels, the auctions and the Cheap Johns, the mountebank, and the marriage-parties, that daily and hourly throng the Grande Place.

Here Bébée, from three years old, had been used to sit beside him. By nature she was as gay as a lark. The people always heard her singing as they passed the garden. The children never found their games so merry as when she danced their rounds with them; and though she dreamed so much out there in the air among the carnations and the roses, or in the long, low work-room in the town, high against the crocketed pinnacles of the cathedral, yet her dreams, if vaguely wistful, were all bright of hue and sunny in their phantasies. Still, Bébée had one sad unsatisfied desire: she wanted to know so much, and she knew nothing.

She did not care for the grand gay people.

When the band played, and the park filled, and the bright little cafés were thronged with pleasure-seekers, and the crowds flocked hither and thither to the woods, to the theatres, to the galleries, to the guinguettes, Bébée, going gravely along with her emptied baskets homeward, envied none of these.

When at Noël the little children hugged their loads of puppets and sugar-plums; when at the Fête Dieu the whole people flocked out be-ribboned and vari-colored like any bed of spring-anemones; when in the merry midsummer the chars-à-bancs trundled away into the forest with laughing loads of students and maidens; when in the rough winters the carriages left furred and jeweled women at the doors of the operas or the palaces—Bébée, going and coming through the city to her flower-stall or lace-work, looked at them all, and never thought of envy or desire.

She had her little hut; she could get her bread; she lived with the flowers; the neighbors were good to her, and now and then, on a saint's day, she too got her day in the woods; it never occurred to her that her lot could be better.

But sometimes sitting, looking at the dark old beauty of the Broodhuis, or at the wondrous carven fronts of other Spanish houses, or at the painted stories of the cathedral windows, or at the quaint colors of the shipping on the quay, or at the long dark aisles of trees that went away through the forest, where her steps had never wandered—sometimes Bébée would get pondering on all this unknown world that lay before and behind and around her, and a sense of her own utter ignorance would steal on her; and she would say to herself, "If only I knew a little—just a very little!"

But it is not easy to know even a very little when you have to work for your bread from sunrise to nightfall, and when none of your friends know how to read or write, and even your old priest is one of a family of peasants, and can just teach you the alphabet, and that is all. For Father Francis could do no more than this; and all his spare time was taken up in digging his cabbage-plot and seeing to his beehives; and the only books that Bébée ever beheld were a few tattered lives of saints that lay moth-eaten on a shelf of his cottage.

But Brussels has stones that are sermons, or rather that are quaint, touching, illuminated legends of the Middle Ages, which those who run may read.

Brussels is a gay little city, that lies as bright within its girdle of woodland as any butterfly that rests upon moss.

The city has its ways and wiles of Paris. It decks itself with white and gold. It has music under its trees and soldiers in its streets, and troops marching and countermarching along its sunny avenues. It has blue and pink, and yellow and green, on its awnings and on its house-fronts. It has a merry open-air life on its pavements at little marble tables before little gay-colored cafés. It has gilded balconies, and tossing flags, and comic operas, and leisurely pleasure-seekers, and tries always to believe and make the world believe that it is Paris in very truth.

But this is only the Brussels of the noblesse and the foreigners.

There is a Brussels that is better than this—a Brussels that belongs to the old burgher-life, to the artists and the craftsmen, to the master-masons of the Moyen-âge, to the same spirit and soul that once filled the free men of Ghent and the citizens of Bruges and the besieged of Leyden, and the blood of Egmont and of Horne.

Down there by the water-side, where the old quaint walls lean over the yellow sluggish stream, and the green barrels of the Antwerp barges swing against the dusky piles of the crumbling bridges.

In the gray square desolate courts of the old palaces, where in cobwebbed galleries and silent chambers the Flemish tapestries drop to pieces.

In the great populous square, where, above the clamorous and rushing crowds, the majestic front of the Maison du Roi frowns against the sun, and the spires and pinnacles of the Burgomaster's gathering-halls tower into the sky in all the fantastic luxuriance of Gothic fancy.

Under the vast shadowy wings of angels in the stillness of the cathedral, across whose sunny aisles some little child goes slowly all alone, laden with lilies for the Feast of the Assumption, till their white glory hides its curly head.

In all strange quaint old-world niches withdrawn from men in silent grass grown corners, where a twelfth-century corbel holds a pot of roses, or a Gothic arch yawns beneath a wool-warehouse, or a water-spout with a grinning faun's head laughs in the grim humor of the Moyen-âge above the bent head of a young lace-worker.

In all these, Brussels, though more worldly than her sisters of Ghent and Bruges, and far more worldly yet than her Teuton cousins of Freiburg and Nürnberg, is still in her own way like as a monkish story mixed up with the Romaunt of the Rose; or rather like some gay French vaudeville, all fashion and jest, illustrated in old Missal manner with helm and hauberk, cope and cowl, praying knights and fighting priests, winged griffins and nimbused saints, flame-breathing dragons and enamored princes, all mingled together in the illuminated colors and the heroical grotesque romance of the Middle Ages.

And it was this side of the city that Bébée knew; and she loved it well, and would not leave it for the market of the Madeleine.

She had no one to tell her anything, and all Antoine had ever been able to say to her concerning the Broodhuis was that it had been there in his father's time; and regarding St. Gudule, that his mother had burned many a candle before its altars for a dead brother who had been drowned off the dunes.

But the child's mind, unled, but not misled, had pondered on these things, and her heart had grown to love them; and perhaps no student of Spanish architecture, no antiquary of Moyen-âge relics, loved St. Gudule and the Broodhuis as little ignorant Bébée did.

There had been a time when great dark, fierce men had builded these things, and made the place beautiful. So much she knew; and the little wistful, untaught brain tried to project itself into those unknown times, and failed, and yet found pleasure in the effort. And Bébée would say to herself as she walked the streets, "Perhaps some one will come some day who will tell me all those things."

Meanwhile, there were the flowers, and she was quite content.

Besides, she knew all the people: the old cobbler, who sat next her, and chattered all day long like a magpie; the tinker, who had come up many a summer night to drink a glass with Antoine; the Cheap John, who cheated everybody else, but who had always given her a toy or a trinket at every Fête Dieu all the summers she had known; the little old woman, sour as a crab, who sold rosaries and pictures of saints, and little waxen Christs upon a tray; the big dogs who pulled the carts in, and lay panting all day under the rush-bottomed chairs on which the egg-wives and the fruit-sellers sat, and knitted, and chaffered; nay, even the gorgeous huissier and the frowning gendarme, who marshaled the folks into order as they went up for municipal registries, or for town-misdemeanors. She knew them all; had known them all ever since she had first trotted in like a little dog at Antoine's heels.

So Bébée stayed there.

It is, perhaps, the most beautiful square in all Northern Europe, with its black timbers and gilded carvings, and blazoned windows, and majestic scutcheons, and fantastic pinnacles. That Bébée did not know, but she loved it, and she sat resolutely in front of the Broodhuis, selling her flowers, smiling, chatting, helping the old woman, counting her little gains, eating her bit of bread at noonday like any other market-girl, but at times glancing up to the stately towers and the blue sky, with a look on her face that made the old tinker and cobbler whisper together, "What does she see there?—the dead people or the angels?"

The truth was that even Bébée herself did not know very surely what she saw—something that was still nearer to her than even this kindly crowd that loved her. That was all she could have said had anybody asked her.

But none did.

No one wanted to hear what the dead said; and for the angels, the tinker and the cobbler were of opinion that one had only too much of them sculptured about everywhere, and shining on all the casements—in reverence be it spoken, of course.

CHAPTER III.

"I REMEMBERED it was your name-day child. Here are half a dozen eggs," said one of the hen-wives; and the little cross woman with the peddler's tray added a waxen St. Agnes, colored red and yellow to the very life no doubt; and the old Cheap John had saved her a cage for the starling; and the tinker had a cream-cheese for her in a vine-leaf, and the sweetmeat-seller brought her a beautiful gilded horn of sugar-plums, and the cobbler had made her actually a pair of shoes—red shoes, beautiful shoes to go to mass in and be a wonder in to all the neighborhood. And they thronged round her, and adored the silver waist-buckles; and when Bébée got fairly to her stall, and traffic began, she thought once more that nobody's feast-day had ever dawned like hers.

When the chimes began to ring all over the city, she could hardly believe that the carillon was not saying its "Laus Deo" with some special meaning in its bells of her.

The morning went by as usual; the noise of the throngs about her like a driving of angry winds, but no more hurting her than the angels on the roof of St. Gudule are hurt by the storm when it breaks.

Hard words, fierce passions, low thoughts, evil deeds, passed by the child without resting on her; her heart was in her flowers, and was like one of them with the dew of daybreak on it.

There were many strangers in the city, and such are always sure to loiter in the Spanish square; and she sold fast and well her lilacs and her roses, and her knots of thyme and sweet-brier.

She was always a little sorry to see them go, her kindly pretty playmates that, nine times out of ten no doubt, only drooped and died in the hands that purchased them, as human souls soil and shrivel in the grasp of the passions that woo them.

The day was a busy one, and brought in good profit. Bébée had no less than fifty sous in her leather pouch when it was over,—a sum of magnitude in the green lane by Laeken.

A few of her moss-roses were still unsold, that was all, when the Ave Maria began ringing over the town and the people dispersed to their homes or their pleasuring.

It was a warm gray evening: the streets were full; there were blossoms in all the balconies, and gay colors in all the dresses. The old tinker put his tools together, and whispered to her,—

"Bébée, as it is your feast-day, come and stroll in St. Hubert's gallery, and I will buy you a little gilt heart, or a sugar-apple stick, or a ribbon, and we can see the puppet-show afterwards, eh?"

But the children were waiting at home: she would not spend the evening in the city; she only thought she would just kneel a moment in the cathedral and say a little prayer or two for a minute—the saints were so good in giving her so many friends.

There is something very touching in the Flemish peasant's relation with his Deity. It is all very vague to him: a jumble of veneration and familiarity, of sanctity and profanity, without any thought of being familiar, or any idea of being profane.

There is a homely poetry, an innocent affectionateness in it, characteristic of the people. He talks to his good angel Michel, and to his friend that dear little Jesus, much as he would talk to the shoemaker over the way or the cooper's child in the doorway.

It is a very unreasonable, foolish, clumsy sort of religion, this theology in wooden shoes; it is half grotesque, half pathetic; the grandmothers pass it on to the grandchildren as they pass the bowl of potatoes round the stove in the long winter nights; it is as silly as possible, but it comforts them as they carry fagots over the frozen canals or wear their eyes blind over the squares of lace; and it has in it the supreme pathos of any perfect confidence, of any utterly childlike and undoubting trust.

This had been taught to Bébée, and she went to sleep every night in the firm belief that the sixteen little angels of the Flemish prayer kept watch and ward over her bed. For the rest, being poetical, as these north folks are not, and having in her—wherever it came from, poor little soul—a warmth of fancy and a spirituality of vision not at all northern, she had mixed up her religion with the fairies of Antoine's stories, and the demons in which the Flemish folks are profound believers, and the flowers into which she put all manner of sentient life, until her religion was a fantastic medley, so entangled that poor Father Francis had given up in despair any attempt to arrange it more correctly. Indeed, being of the peasantry himself, he was not so very full sure in his own mind that demons were not bodily presences, quite as real and often much more tangible than saints. Anyway, he let her alone; and she believed in the goodness of God as she believed in the shining of the sun.

People looked after her as she went through the twisting, picture-like streets, where sunlight fell still between the peaked high roofs, and lamps were here and there lit in the bric-a-brac shops and the fruit-stalls.

Her little muslin cap blew back like the wings of a white butterfly. Her sunny hair caught the last sun-rays. Her feet were fair in the brown wooden shoes. Under the short woolen skirts the grace of her pretty limbs moved freely. Her broad silver clasps shone like a shield, and she was utterly unconscious that any one looked; she was simply and gravely intent on reaching St. Gudule to say her one prayer and not keep the children waiting.

Some one leaning idly over a balcony in the street that is named after Mary of Burgundy saw her going thus. He left the balcony and went down his stairs and followed her.

The sun-dazzle on the silver had first caught his sight; and then he had looked downward at the pretty feet.

These are the chances women call Fate.

Bébée entered the cathedral. It was quite empty. Far away at the west end there was an old custodian asleep on a bench, and a woman kneeling. That was all.

Bébée made her salutations to the high altar, and stole on into the chapel of the Saint Sacrament; it was that one that she loved best.

She said her prayer, and thanked the saints for all their gifts and goodness, her clasped hand against her silver shield, her basket on the pavement by her, abovehead the sunset rays streaming purple and crimson and golden through the painted windows that are the wonder of the world.

When her prayer was done she still kneeled there; her head thrown back to watch the light, her hands clasped still, and on her upturned face the look that made the people say, "What does she see?—the angels or the dead?"

She forgot everything. She forgot the cherries at home, and the children even. She was looking upward at the stories of the painted panes; she was listening to the message of the dying sun-rays; she was feeling vaguely, wistfully, unutterably the tender beauty of the sacred place and the awful wonder of the world in which she with her sixteen years was all alone, like a little blue corn-flower among the wheat that goes for grist and the barley that makes men drunk.

For she was alone, though she had so many friends. Quite alone sometimes; for God had been cruel to her, and had made her a lark without song.

When the sun faded and the beautiful casements lost all glow and meaning, Bébée rose with a startled look—had she been dreaming?—was it night?—would the children be sorry, and go supperless to bed?

"Have you a rosebud left to sell to me?" a man's voice said not far off; it was low and sweet, as became the Sacrament Chapel.

Bébée looked up; she did not quite know what she saw: only dark eyes smiling into hers.

By the instinct of habit she sought in her basket and found three moss-roses. She held them out to him.

"I do not sell flowers here, but I will *give* them to you," she said, in her pretty grave childish fashion.

"I often want flowers," said the stranger, as he took the buds. "Where do you sell yours?—in the market?"

"In the Grande Place."

"Will you tell me your name, pretty one?"

"I am Bébée."

There were people coming into the church. The bells were booming abovehead for vespers. There was a shuffle of chairs and a stir of feet. Boys in white went to and fro, lighting the candles. Great clouds of shadow drifted up into the roof and hid the angels.

She nodded her little head to him.

"Good-night; I cannot stay. I have a cake at home to-night, and the children are waiting."

"Ah! that is important, no doubt, indeed. Will you buy some more cakes for the children from me?"

He slid a gold piece in her hand. She looked at it in amaze. In the green lanes by Laeken no one ever saw gold. Then she gave it him back.

"I will not take money in church, nor anywhere, except what the flowers are worth. Good-night."

He followed her, and held back the heavy oak door for her, and went out into the air with her.

It was dark already, but in the square there was still the cool bright primrose-colored evening light.

Bébée's wooden shoes went pattering down the sloping and uneven stones. Her little gray figure ran quickly through the deep shade cast from the towers and walls. Her dreams had drifted away. She was thinking of the children and the cake.

"You are in such a hurry because of the cake?" said her new customer, as he followed her.

Bébée looked back at him with a smile in her blue eyes.

"Yes—they will be waiting, you know, and there are cherries too."

"It is a grand day with you, then?"

"It is my fête day: I am sixteen."

She was proud of this. She told it to the very dogs in the street.

"Ah!—you feel old, I dare say?"

"Oh, quite old! They cannot call me a child any more."

"Of course not; it would be ridiculous. Are those presents in your basket?"

"Yes, every one of them." She paused a moment to lift the dead vine-leaves, and show him the beautiful shining red shoes. "Look!—old Gringoire gave me these. I shall wear them at mass next Sunday. I never had a pair of shoes in my life."

"But how will you wear shoes without stockings?"

It was a snake cast into her Eden.

She had never thought of it.

"Perhaps I can save money and buy some," she answered, after a sad little pause. "But that I could not do till next year. They would cost several francs, I suppose."

"Unless a good fairy gives them to you?"

Bébée smiled; fairies were real things to her—relations indeed. She did not imagine that he spoke in jest.

"Sometimes I pray very much and things come," she said softly. "When the Gloire de Dijon was cut back too soon one summer, and never blossomed, and we all thought it was dead, I prayed all day long for it, and never thought of anything else; and by autumn it was all in new leaf, and now its flowers are finer than ever."

"But you watered it whilst you prayed, I suppose?"

The sarcasm escaped her.

She was wondering to herself whether it would be vain and wicked to pray for a pair of stockings: she thought she would go and ask Father Francis.

By this time they were in the Rue Royale, and half-way down it. The lamps were lighted. A regiment was marching up it with a band playing. The windows were open, and people were laughing and singing in some of them. The light caught the white and gilded fronts of the houses. The pleasure-seeking crowds loitered along in the warmth of the evening.

Bébée, suddenly roused from her thoughts by the loud challenge of the military music, looked round on the stranger, and motioned him back.

"Sir,—I do not know you,—why should you come with me? Do not do it, please. You make me talk, and that makes me late."

And she pushed her basket farther on her arm, and nodded to him, and ran off—as fleetly as a hare through fern—among the press of the people.

"To-morrow, little one," he answered her with a careless smile, and let her go unpursued. Above, from the open casement of a café, some young men and some painted women leaned out, and threw sweetmeats at him, as in carnival-time.

"A new model,—that pretty peasant?" they asked him.

He laughed in answer, and went up the steps to join them; he dropped the moss-roses as he went, and trod on them, and did not wait.

CHAPTER IV.

BEBEE ran home as fast as her feet would take her.

The children were all gathered about her gate in the dusky dewy evening; they met her with shouts of welcome and reproach intermingled; they had been watching for her since first the sun had grown low and red, and now the moon was risen.

But they forgave her when they saw the splendor of her presents, and she showered out among them Père Melchior's horn of comfits.

They dashed into the hut; they dragged the one little table out among the flowers; the cherries and cake were spread on it; and the miller's wife had given a big jug of milk, and Father Francis himself had sent some honeycomb.

The early roses were full of scent in the dew; the great gillyflowers breathed out fragrance in the dusk; the goat came and nibbled the sweet-brier unrebuked; the children repeated the Flemish bread-grace, with clasped hands and reverent eyes—"Oh, dear little Jesus, come and sup with us, and bring your beautiful Mother too; we will not forget you are God." Then, that said, they ate, and drank, and laughed, and picked cherries from each other's mouths like little blackbirds; the big white dog gnawed a crust at their feet; old Krebs, who had a fiddle, and could play it, came out and trilled them rude and ready Flemish tunes, such as Teniers or Mieris might have jumped to before an ale-house at the Kermesse; Bébée and the children joined hands, and danced round together in the broad white moonlight, on the grass by the water-side; the idlers came and sat about, the women netting or spinning, and the men smoking a pipe before bed-time; the rough hearty Flemish bubbled like a brook in gossip, or rung like a horn over a jest; Bébée and the children, tired of their play, grew quiet, and chanted together the "Ave Maria Stella Virginis;" a nightingale among the willows sang to the sleeping swans.

All was happy, quiet, homely; lovely also in its simple way.

They went early to their beds, as people must do who rise at dawn.

Bébée leaned out a moment from her own little casement ere she too went to rest.

Through an open lattice there sounded the murmur of some little child's prayer; the wind sighed among the willows; the nightingales sang on in the dark—all was still.

Hard work awaited her on the morrow, and on all the other days of the year.

She was only a little peasant,—she must sweep,

and spin, and dig, and delve, to get daily her bit of black bread,—but that night she was as happy as a little princess in a fairy tale; happy in her playmates, in her flowers, in her sixteen years, in her red shoes, in her silver buckles, because she was half a woman; happy in the dewy leaves, in the singing birds, in the hush of the night, in the sense of rest, in the fragrance of flowers, in the drifting changes of moon and cloud; happy because she was half a woman, because she was half a poet, because she was wholly a poet.

"Oh, dear swans, how good it is to be sixteen! —how good it is to live at all!—do you not tell the willows so?" said Bébée to the gleam of silver under the dark leaves by the water's side, which showed her where her friends were sleeping, with their snowy wings closed over their stately heads, and the veiled gold and ruby of their eyes.

The swans did not awake to answer.

Only the nightingale answered from the willows, with Desdemona's song.

But Bébée had never heard of Desdemona, and the willows had no sigh for her.

"Good-night!" she said, softly, to all the green dewy sleeping world, and then she lay down and slept herself.—The nightingale sang on, and the willows trembled.

CHAPTER V.

"IF I could save a centime a day, I could buy a pair of stockings this time next year," thought Bébée, locking her shoes with her other treasures in her drawer the next morning, and taking her broom and pail to wash down her little palace.

But a centime a day is a great deal in Brabant, when one has not always enough for bare bread, and when, in the long chill winter, one must weave thread lace all through the short daylight for next to nothing at all; for there are so many women in Brabant, and every one of them, young or old, can make lace, and if one do not like the pitiful wage, one may leave it and go and die, for what the master lace-makers care or know; there will always be enough, many more than enough, to twist the thread round the bobbins, and weave the bridal veils, and the trains for the courts.

"And besides, if I can save a centime, the Varnhart children ought to have it," thought Bébée, as she swept the dust together. It was so selfish of her to be dreaming about a pair of stockings, when those little things often went for days on a stew of nettles.

So she looked at her own pretty feet,—pretty, and slender, and arched, rosy, and fair, and uncramped by the pressure of leather,—and resigned her day-dream with a brave heart, as she put up her broom and went out to weed, and hoe, and trim, and prune the garden that had been for once neglected the night before.

"One could not move half so easily in stockings," she thought with true philosophy as she worked among the black fresh sweet-smelling mould, and kissed a rose now and then as she passed one.

When she got into the city that day, her rush-bottomed chair, which was always left upside down in case rain should fall in the night, was set ready for her, and on its seat was a gay, gilded box, such as rich people give away full of bonbons.

Bébée stood and looked from the box to the Broodhuis, from the Broodhuis to the box; she glanced around, but no one had come there so early as she, except the tinker, who was busy quarreling with his wife and letting his smelting fire burn a hole in his breeches.

"The box was certainly for her, since it was set upon her chair?"—Bébée pondered a moment; then little by little opened the lid.

Within, on a nest of rose-satin, were two pair of silk stockings!—Real silk!—with the prettiest clocks worked up their sides in color!

Bébée gave a little scream, and stood still, the blood hot in her cheeks; no one heard her, the tinker's wife, who alone was near, having just wished Heaven to send a judgment on her husband, was busy putting out his smoking small-clothes. It is a way that women and wives have, and they never see the bathos of it.

The Place filled gradually.

The customary crowds gathered. The business of the day began underneath the multitudinous tones of the chiming bells. Bébée's business began too; she put the box behind her with a beating heart, and tied up her flowers.

It was the fairies, of course!—but they had never set a rush-bottomed chair on its legs before, and this action of theirs frightened her.

It was rather an empty morning. She sold little, and there was the more time to think.

About an hour after noon, a voice addressed her,—

"Have you more moss-roses for me?"

Bébée looked up with a smile, and found some. It was her companion of the cathedral. She had thought much of the red shoes and the silver clasps, but she had thought nothing at all of him.

"You are not too proud to be paid to-day?" he said, giving her a silver franc—he would not alarm her with any more gold; she thanked him, and slipped it in her little leathern pouch, and went on sorting some clove-pinks.

"You do not seem to remember me?" he said, with a little sadness.

"Oh, I remember you," said Bébée, lifting her

frank eyes. "But you know I speak to so many people, and they are all nothing to me."

"Who is anything to you?" It was softly and insidiously spoken, but it awoke no echo.

"Varnhart's children," she answered him, instantly. "And old Annémie by the wharfside—and Tambour—and Antoine's grave—and the starling—and, of course, above all, the flowers."

"And the fairies, I suppose?—though they do nothing for you."

She looked at him eagerly,—

"They have done something to-day. I have found a box, and some stockings—such beautiful stockings! Silk ones! Is it not very odd?"

"It is more odd they should have forgotten you so long. May I see them?"

"I cannot show them to you now. Those ladies are going to buy. But you can see them later—if you wait."

"I will wait and paint the Broodhuis."

"So many people do that; you are a painter then?"

"Yes—in a way."

He sat down on an edge of the stall, and spread his things there, and sketched, whilst the traffic went on around them. He was very many years older than she; handsome, with a dark, and changeful, and listless face; he wore brown velvet, and had a red ribbon at his throat; he looked a little as Egmont might have done when wooing Claire.

Bébée, as she sold the flowers and took the change fifty times in the hour, glanced at him now and then, and watched the movements of his hands—she could not have told why.

Always among men and women, always in the crowds of the streets, people were nothing to her; she went through them as through a field of standing corn,—only in the field she would have tarried for poppies, and in the town she tarried for no one.

She dealt with men as with women, simply, truthfully, frankly, with the innocent fearlessness of a child. When they told her she was pretty, she smiled; it was just as they said that her flowers were sweet.

But this man's hands moved so swiftly; and as she saw her Broodhuis growing into color and form beneath them she could not choose but look now and then, and twice she gave her change wrong.

He spoke to her rarely, and sketched on and on in rapid bold strokes the quaint graces and massive richness of the Maison du Roi.

There is no crowd so busy in Brabant that it will not find leisure to stare. The Fleming or the Walloon has nothing of the Frenchman's courtesy; he is rough and rude; he remains a peasant even when town-bred, and the surly insolence of the "Gueux" is in him still. He is kindly to his fellows, though not to beasts; he is shrewd, patient, thrifty, industrious, and good in very many ways, but civil never.

A good score of them left off their occupations and clustered round the painter, staring, chattering, pushing, pointing, as though a brush had never been seen in all the land of Rubens.

Bébée, ashamed of her people, got up from her chair and rebuked them.

"Oh, men of Brussels; fie then for shame!" she called to them as clearly as a robin sings. "Did never you see a drawing before? and are there not saints and martyrs enough to look at in the galleries?—and have you never some better thing to do than to gape wide-mouthed at a stranger? What laziness—ah! just worthy of a people who sleep and smoke while their dogs work for them! Go away, all of you; look, there comes the gendarme—it will be the worse for you. Sir, sit under my stall; they will not dare trouble you then."

He moved under the awning, thanking her with a smile; and the people, laughing, shuffled unwillingly aside and let him paint on in peace. It was only little Bébée, but they had spoilt the child from her infancy, and were used to obey her.

The painter took a long time. He set about it with the bold ease of one used to all the intricacies of form and color, and he had the skill of a master. But he spent more than half the time looking idly at the humors of the populace or watching how the treasures of Bébée's garden went away one by one in the hands of strangers.

Meanwhile, ever and again, sitting on the edge of her stall, with his colors and brushes tossed out on the board, he talked to her, and, with the soft imperceptible skill of long practice in those arts, he drew out the details of her little simple life.

There were not always people to buy, and whilst she rested and sheltered the flowers from the sun she answered him willingly, and in one of her longer rests showed him the wonderful stockings.

"Do you think it *could* be the fairies?" she asked him a little doubtfully.

It was easy to make her believe any fantastical nonsense; but her fairies were ethereal divinities. She could scarcely believe that they had laid that box on her chair.

"Impossible to doubt it!" he replied, unhesitatingly. "Given a belief in fairies at all, why should there be any limit to what they can do? It is the same with the saints, is it not?"

"Yes," said Bébée, thoughtfully.

The saints were mixed up in her imagination with the fairies in an intricacy that would have defied the best reasonings of Father Francis.

"Well, then, you will wear the stockings, will you not? Only, believe me, your feet are far prettier without them."

Bébée laughed happily, and took another peep in the cosy rose-satin nest. But her little face had a certain perplexity. Suddenly she turned on him.

"Did not *you* put them there?"

"I?—never!"

"Are you quite sure?"

"Quite; but why ask?"

"Because," said Bébée, shutting the box resolutely and pushing it a little away, "because I would not take it if you did. You are a stranger, and a present is a debt, so Antoine always said."

"Why take a present then from the Varnhart children, or your old friend who gave you the clasps?"

"Ah, that is very different. When people are very, very poor, equally poor, the one with the other, little presents that they save for and make with such a difficulty are just things that are a pleasure; sacrifices; like your sitting up with a sick person at night, and then she sits up with you another year when you want it. Do you not know?"

"I know you talk very prettily. But why should you not take any one else's present, though he may not be poor?"

"Because I could not return it."

"Could you not?"

The smile in his eyes dazzled her a little; it was so strange, and yet had so much light in it; but she did not understand him one whit.

"No; how could I?" she said, earnestly. "If I were to save for two years, I could not get francs enough to buy anything worth giving back; and I should be so unhappy, thinking of the debt of it always. Do tell me if you put those stockings there?"

"No;" he looked at her, and the trivial lie

faltered and died away; the eyes, clear as crystal, questioned him so innocently.

"Well, if I did?" he said, frankly, "you wished for them; what harm was there? Will you be so cruel as to refuse them from me?"

The tears sprang into Bébée's eyes. She was sorry to lose the beautiful box, but more sorry he had lied to her.

"It was very kind and good," she said, regretfully. "But I cannot think why you should have done it, as you had never known me at all. And, indeed, I could not take them, because Antoine would not let me if he were alive; and if I gave you a flower every day all the year round I should not pay you the worth of them—it would be quite impossible; and why should you tell me falsehoods about such a thing? A falsehood is never a thing for a man."

She shut the box and pushed it towards him, and turned to the selling of her bouquets. Her voice shook a little as she tied up a bunch of mignonette and told the price of it.

Those beautiful stockings! why had she ever seen them, and why had he told her a lie?

It made her heart heavy. For the first time in her brief life the Broodhuis seemed to frown between her and the sun.

Undisturbed, he painted on and did not look at her.

The day was nearly done. The people began to scatter. The shadows grew very long. He painted, not glancing once elsewhere than at his study. Bébée's baskets were quite empty.

She rose, and lingered, and regarded him wistfully: he was angered; perhaps she had been rude? Her little heart failed her.

If he would only look up!—

But he did not look up; he kept his handsome dark face studiously over the canvas of the Broodhuis. She would have seen a smile in his eyes if he had lifted them; but he never raised his lids.

Bébée hesitated: take the stockings she would not; but perhaps she had refused them too roughly. She wished so that he would look up and save her speaking first; but he knew what he was about too warily and well to help her thus.

She waited awhile, then took one little red moss-rosebud that she had saved all day in a corner of her basket, and held it out to him frankly, shyly, as a peace-offering.

"Was I rude? I did not mean to be. But I cannot take the stockings; and why did you tell me that falsehood?"

He took the rosebud and rose too, and smiled; but he did not meet her eyes.

"Let us forget the whole matter; it is not worth a sou. If you do not take the box, leave it; it is of no use to me."

"I cannot take it."

She knew she was doing right. How was it that he could make her feel as though she were acting wrongly?

"Leave it then, I say. You are not the first woman, my dear, who has quarreled with a wish fulfilled. It is a way your sex has of rewarding gods and men. Here, you old witch—here is a treasure-trove for you. You can sell it for ten francs in the town anywhere."

As he spoke he tossed the casket and the stockings in it to an old decrepit woman, who was passing by with a baker's cart drawn by a dog; and, not staying to heed her astonishment, gathered his colors and easel together.

The tears swam in Bébée's eyes as she saw the box whirled through the air.

She had done right—she was sure she had done right.

He was a stranger, and she could never have repaid him; but he made her feel herself wayward and ungrateful, and it was hard to see the beautiful fairy gift borne away forever by the chuckling, hobbling, greedy old baker's woman. If he had only taken it himself, she would have been glad then to have been brave and to have done her duty.

But it was not in his design that she should be glad.

He saw her tears, but he seemed not to see them.

"Good-night, Bébée," he said carelessly, as he sauntered aside from her. "Good-night, my dear. To-morrow I will finish my painting; but I will not offend you by any more gifts."

Bébée lifted her drooped head, and looked him

in the eyes eagerly, with a certain sturdy resolve and timid wistfulness intermingled in her look.

"Sir,—see, you speak to me quite wrongly," she said with a quick accent, that had pride as well as pain in it. "Say it was kind to bring me what I wished for—yes, it was kind, I know; but you never saw me till last night, and I cannot tell even your name; and it is very wrong to lie to any one, even to a little thing like me; and I am only Bébée, and cannot give you anything back, because I have only just enough to feed myself and the starling, and not always that in winter. I thank you very much for what you wished to do; but if I had taken those things, I think you would have thought me very mean and full of greed; and Antoine always said, 'Do not take what you cannot pay—not ever what you cannot pay—that is the way to walk with pure feet.' Perhaps I spoke ill, because they spoil me, and they say I am too swift to say my mind. But I am not thankless—not thankless, indeed—it is only I could not take what I cannot pay. That is all. You are angry still—not now—no?"

There was anxiety in the pleading. What did it matter to her what a stranger thought?

And yet Bébée's heart was heavy as he laughed a little coldly, and bade her good-day, and left her alone to go out of the city homewards. A sense of having done wrong weighed on her; of having been rude and ungrateful.

She had no heart for the children that evening.

Mère Krebs was sitting out before her door shelling peas, and called to her to come in and have a drop of coffee. Krebs had come in from Vilvöorde fair, and brought a stock of rare good berries with him. But Bébée thanked her, and went on to her own garden to work.

She had always liked to sit out on the quaint wooden steps of the mill and under the red shadow of the sails, watching the swallows flutter to and fro in the sunset, and hearing the droll frogs croak in the rushes, while the old people told her tales of the time of how in their babyhood they had run out, fearful yet fascinated, to see the beautiful Scots Grays flash by in the murky night, and the endless line of guns and caissons crawl black as a snake through the summer dust and the trampled corn, going out past the woods to Waterloo.

But to-night she had no fancy for it: she wanted to be alone with the flowers.

Though, to be sure, they had been very heartless when Antoine's coffin had gone past them, still they had sympathy; the daisies smiled at her with their golden eyes, and the roses dropped tears on her hand, just as her mood might be; the flowers were closer friends, after all, than any human souls; and besides, she could say so much to them!

Flowers belong to fairy-land; the flowers and the birds, and the butterflies, are all that the world has kept of its Golden Age; the only perfectly beautiful things on earth, joyous, innocent, half-divine, useless, say they who are wiser than God.

Bébée went home and worked among her flowers.

A little laborious figure, with her petticoats twisted high, and her feet wet with the night dews, and her back bowed to the hoeing and clipping and raking among the blossoming plants.

"How late you are working to-night, Bébée!" one or two called out, as they passed the gate. She looked up and smiled; but went on working while the white moon rose.

She did not know what ailed her.

She went to bed without supper, leaving her bit of bread and bowl of goat's milk to make a meal for the fowls in the morning.

"Little ugly, shameful, naked feet!" she said to them, sitting on the edge of her mattress, and looking at them in the moonlight. They were very pretty feet, and would not have been half so pretty in silk hose and satin shoon; but she did not know that: he had told her she wanted those vanities.

She sat still a long while, her rosy feet swaying to and fro like two roses that grow on one stalk and hang down in the wind. The little lattice was open; the sweet and dusky garden was beyond; there was a hand's breadth of sky, in which a single star was shining; the leaves of the vine hid all the rest.

But for once she saw none of it.

She only saw the black Broodhuis; the red and gold sunset overhead; the gray stones, with the fallen rose-leaves and crushed fruits; and in the shadows two dark, reproachful eyes, that looked at hers.

Had she been ungrateful?

The little tender, honest heart of her was troubled and oppressed. For once, that night she slept ill.

CHAPTER VI.

ALL the next day she sat under the yellow awning, but she sat alone.

It was market-day; there were many strangers. Flowers were in demand. The copper pieces were ringing against one another all the hours through in her leathern bag. The cobbler was in such good humor that he forgot to quarrel with his wife. The fruit was in such plenty that they gave her a leaf-full of white and red currants for her noonday dinner. And the people split their sides at the Cheap John's jokes; he was so droll. No one saw the leaks in his kettles or the hole in his bellows, or the leg that was lacking to his milking-stool.

Everybody was gay and merry that day. But Bébée's blue eyes looked wistfully over the throng, and did not find what they sought. Somehow the day seemed dull, and the square empty.

The stones and the timbers around seemed more than ever full of a thousand stories that they would not tell her because she knew nothing, and was only Bébée.

She had never known a dull hour before. She,

a little bright, industrious, gay thing, whose hands were always full of work, and whose head was always full of fancies, even in the grimmest winter-time, when she wove the lace in the gray, chilly work-room, with the frost on the casements, and the mice running out in their hunger over the bare brick floor.

That bare room was a sad enough place sometimes, when the old women would bewail how they starved on the pittance they gained, and the young women sighed for their aching heads and their failing eyesight, and the children dropped great tears on the bobbins, because they had come out without a crust to break their fast.

She had been sad there often for others, but she had never been dull—not with this unfamiliar, desolate, dreary dullness, that seemed to take all the mirth out of the busy life around her, and all the color out of the blue sky above. Why, she had no idea herself. She wondered if she were going to be ill; she had never been ill in her life, being strong as a little bird that has never known cage or captivity.

When the day was done, Bébée gave a quick sigh as she looked across the square. She had so wanted to tell him that she was not ungrateful; and she had a little moss-rose ready, with a sprig of sweet-brier, and a tiny spray of maiden-hair fern that grew under the willows, which she had kept covered up with a leaf of sycamore all the day long.

No one would have it now.

The child went out of the place sadly, as the carillon rang. There was only the moss-rose in her basket, and the red and white currants that had been given her for her dinner.

She went along the twisting, many-colored, quaintly-fashioned streets, till she came to the water-side.

It is very ancient there still; there are all manner of old buildings, black and brown and gray, peaked roofs, gabled windows, arched doors, crumbling bridges, twisted galleries leaning to touch the dark surface of the canal, dusky wharves crowded with barrels, and bales, and cattle, and timber, and all the various freightage that the good ships come and go with all the year round, to and from the Zuyder-Zee, and the Baltic water, and the wild Northumbrian shores, and the iron-bound Scottish headlands, and the pretty gray Norman seaports, and the white sandy dunes of Holland, with the toy towns and the straight poplar-trees.

Bébée was fond of watching the brigs and barges, that looked so big to her, with their national flags flying, and their tall masts standing thick as grass, and their tawny sails flapping in the wind, and about them the sweet, strong smell of that strange, unknown thing, the sea.

Sometimes the sailors would talk with her; sometimes some old salt, sitting astride of a cask, would tell her a mariner's tale of far-away lands and mysteries of the deep; sometimes some curly-headed cabin-boy would give her a shell or a plume of sea-weed, and try and make her understand what the wonderful wild water was like, which was not quiet and sluggish and dusky as this canal was, but was forever changing and moving, and curling and leaping, and making itself now blue as her eyes, now black as that thunder-cloud, now white as the snow that the winter wind tossed, now pearl-hued and opaline as the convolvulus that blew in her own garden.

And Bébée would listen, with the shell in her lap, and try to understand, and gaze at the ships and then at the sky beyond them, and try to figure to herself those strange countries to which these ships were always going, and saw in fancy all the blossoming orchard province of green France, and all the fir-clothed hills and rushing rivers of the snow-locked Swedish shore, and saw too, doubtless, many lands that had no place at all except in dream-land, and were more beautiful even than the beauty of the earth, as poets' countries are, to their own sorrow oftentimes.

But this dull day Bébée did not go down upon the wharf; she did not want the sailors' tales; she saw the masts and the bits of bunting that streamed from them, and they made her restless, which they had never done before.

Instead she went in at a dark old door and climbed up a steep staircase that went up and up, as though she were mounting St. Gudule's belfry towers; and at the top of it entered a little chamber in the roof, where one square unglazed hole that served for light looked out upon the canal, with all its crowded craft, from the dainty schooner-yacht, fresh as gilding and holy-stone could make her, that was running for pleasure to the Scheldt, to the rude, clumsy coal-barge, black as night, that bore the rough diamonds of Belgium to the snow-buried roofs of Christiania and Stromstad.

In the little dark attic there was a very old woman in a red petticoat and a high cap, who sat against the window, and pricked out lace patterns with a pin, on thick paper. She was eighty-five years old, and could hardly keep body and soul together.

Bébée, running to her, kissed her.

"Oh, mother Annémie, look here! Beautiful red and white currants, and a roll; I saved them for you. They are the first currants we have seen this year. Me? oh, for me, I have eaten more than are good! You know I pick fruit like a sparrow, always. Dear mother Annémie, are you better? Are you quite sure you are better to-day?"

The little old withered woman, brown as a walnut and meagre as a rush, took the currants, and smiled with a childish glee, and began to eat them, blessing the child with each crumb she broke off the bread.

"Why had you not a grandmother of your own, my little one?" she mumbled. "How good you would have been to her, Bébée!"

"Yes," said Bébée seriously, but her mind could

not grasp the idea. It was easier for her to believe the fanciful lily-parentage of Antoine's stories. "How much work have you done, Annémie? Oh, all that? all that? But there is enough for a week. You work too early and too late, you dear Annémie."

"Nay, Bébée, when one has to get one's bread that cannot be. But I am afraid my eyes are failing. That rose now, is it well done?"

"Beautifully done. Would the Baës take them if they were not? You know he is one that cuts every centime in four pieces."

"Ah! sharp enough, sharp enough—that is true. But I am always afraid of my eyes. I do not see the flags out there so well as I used to do."

"Because the sun is so bright, Annémie; that is all. I myself, when I have been sitting all day in the Place in the light, the flowers look pale to me. And you know it is not age with *me*, Annémie?"

The old woman and the young girl laughed together at that droll idea.

"You have a merry heart, dear little one," said old Annémie. "The saints keep it to you always."

"May I tidy the room a little?"

"To be sure, dear, and thank you too. I have not much time, you see; and somehow my back aches badly when I stoop."

"And it is so damp here for you, over all that water!" said Bébée as she swept and dusted and set to rights the tiny place, and put in a little broken pot a few sprays of honeysuckle and rosemary that she had brought with her. "It is so damp here. You should have come and lived in my hut with me, Annémie, and sat out under the vine all day, and looked after the chickens for me when I was in the town. They are such mischievous little souls; as soon as my back is turned one or other is sure to push through the roof, and get out among the flowerbeds. Will you never change your mind, and live with me, Annémie? I am sure you would be happy, and the starling says your name quite plain, and he is such a funny bird to talk to; you never would tire of him. Will you never come? It is so bright there, and green and sweet-smelling; and to think you never even have seen it!—and the swans and all,—it is a shame."

"No, dear," said old Annémie, eating her last bunch of currants. "You have said so so often, and you are good and mean it, that I know. But I could not leave the water. It would kill me. Out of this window you know I saw my Jeannot's brig go away—away—away—till the masts were lost in the mists. Going with iron to Norway; the Fleur d'Epine of this town, a good ship, and a sure, and her mate; and as proud as might be, and with a little blest Mary in lead round his throat. She was to be back in port in eight months, bringing timber. Eight months—that brought Easter-time. But she never came. Never, never, never, you know. I sat here watching them come and go, and my child sickened and died, and the summer passed, and the autumn, and all the while I looked —looked—looked; for the brigs are all much alike; and only her I always saw as soon as she hove in sight (because he tied a hank of flax to her mizzen mast); and when he was home safe and sound I spun the hank into hose for him; that was a fancy of his, and for eleven voyages, one on another, he had never missed to tie the flax nor I to spin the hose. But the hank of flax I never saw this time; nor the brave brig; nor my good man with his sunny blue eyes. Only one day in winter, when the great blocks of ice were smashing hither and thither, a coaster came in and brought tidings of how off in the Danish waters they had come on a waterlogged brig, and had boarded her, and had found her empty, and her hull riven in two, and her crew all drowned and dead beyond any manner of doubt. And on her stern there was her name painted white, the Fleur d'Epine, of Brussels, as plain as name could be; and that was all we ever knew: what evil had struck her, or how they had perished, nobody ever told. Only the coaster brought that bit of beam away, with the Fleur d'Epine writ clear upon it. But you see I never *know* my man is dead. Any day—who can say?—any one of those ships may bring him aboard of her, and he may leap out on the wharf there, and come running up the stairs as he used to do, and cry, in his merry voice, 'Annémie, Annémie, here is more flax to spin, here is more hose to weave!' For that was always his homeward word; no matter whether he had had fair weather or foul, he always knotted the flax to his masthead. So you see, dear, I could not leave here. For what if he came and found me away? He would say it was an odd fashion of mourning for him. And I could not do without the window, you know. I can watch all the brigs come in; and I can smell the shipping smell that I have loved all the days of my life; and I can see the lads heaving, and climbing, and furling, and mending their bits of canvas, and hauling their flags up and down. And then who can say? —the sea never took him, I think—I think I shall hear his voice before I die. For they do say that God is good."

Bébée, sweeping very noiselessly, listened, and her eyes grew wistful and wondering. She had heard the story a thousand times; always in different words, but always the same little tale, and she knew how old Annémie was deaf to all the bells that tolled the time, and blind to all the whiteness of her hair and all the wrinkles of her face, and only thought of her sea-slain lover as he had been in the days of her youth.

But this afternoon the familiar history had a new patheticalness for her, and as the old soul put aside with her palsied hand the square of canvas that screened the casement, and looked out, with her old dim sad eyes strained in the longing that God never answered, Bébée felt a strange chill at her own heart, and wondered to herself,—

"What can it be to care for another creature like that? It must be so terrible, and yet it must be beautiful too. Does every one suffer like that?"

She did not speak at all as she finished sweeping the bricks, and went down-stairs for a metal cruche full of water, and set over a little charcoal on the stove the old woman's brass soup-kettle with her supper of stewing cabbage.

Annémie did not hear or notice; she was still looking out of the hole in the wall on to the masts, and the sails, and the water.

It was twilight.

From the barges and brigs there came the smell of the sea. The sailors were shouting to each other. The craft were crowded close, and lost in the growing darkness. On the other side of the canal the belfries were ringing for vespers.

"Eleven voyages one and another, and he never forgot to tie the flax to the mast," Annémie murmured, with her old wrinkled face leaning out into the gray air. "It used to fly there,—one could see it coming up half a mile off,—just a pale-yellow flake on the wind, like a tress of my hair, he would say. No, no, I could not go away; he may come to-night, to-morrow, any time; he is not drowned, not my man; he was all I had, and God is good, they say."

Bébée listened and looked; then kissed the old shaking hand and took up the lace patterns and went softly out of the room without speaking.

When old Annémie watched at the window it

was useless to seek for any word or sign of her; people said that she had never been quite right in her brain since that fatal winter noon sixty years before, when the coaster had brought into port the broken beam of the good brig Fleur d'Epine.

Bébée did not know about that, nor heed whether her wits were right or not.

She had known the old creature in the lace-room where Annémie pricked out designs, and she had conceived a great regard and sorrow for her; and when Annémie had become too ailing and aged to go herself any longer to the lace-maker's place, Bébée had begged leave for her to have the patterns at home, and had carried them to and fro for her for the last three or four years, doing many other little useful services for the lone old soul as well—services which Annémie hardly perceived, she had grown so used to them, and her feeble intelligence was so sunk in the one absorbing idea that she must watch all the days through and all the years through for the coming of the dead man and the lost brig.

Bébée put the lace patterns in her basket, and trotted home, her sabots clattering on the stones.

"What is must be to care for any one like that!" she thought, and by some vague association of thought that she could not have pursued, she lifted the leaves and looked at the moss-rose-bud.

It was quite dead.

CHAPTER VII.

AS she got clear of the city and out on her country road, a shadow fell across her in the evening light.

"Have you had a good day, little one?" asked a voice that made her stop with a curious vague expectancy and pleasure.

"It is you!" she said, with a little cry, as she saw her friend of the silk stockings leaning on a gate midway in the green and solitary road that leads to Laeken.

"Yes, it is I," he answered, as he joined her. "Have you forgiven me, Bébée?"

She looked at him with frank, appealing eyes, like those of a child in fault.

"Oh, I did not sleep all night," she said, simply. "I thought I had been rude and ungrateful, and I could not be sure I had done right, though to have done otherwise would certainly have been wrong."

He laughed.

"Well, that is a clearer deduction than is to be drawn from most moral uncertainties. Do not think twice about the matter, my dear. I have not, I assure you."

"No!"

She was a little disappointed. It seemed such an immense thing to her; and she had lain awake all the night, turning it about in her little brain, and appealing vainly for help in it to the sixteen sleep-angels.

"No, indeed. And where are you going so fast, as if those wooden shoes of yours were sandals of Mercury?"

"Mercury—is that a shoemaker?"

"No, my dear. He did a terrible bit of cobbling once, when he made Woman. But he did not shoe her feet with swiftness that I know of; she only runs away to be run after, and if you do not pursue her, she comes back—always."

Bébée did not understand at all.

"I thought God made women," she said, a little awe-stricken.

"You call it God. People three thousand years ago called it Mercury or Hermes. Both mean the same thing,—mere words to designate an unknown quality. Where are you going? Does your home lie here?"

"Yes, onward, quite far onward," said Bébée, wondering that he had forgotten all she had told him the day before about her hut, her garden, and her neighbors. "You did not come and finish your picture to-day: why was that? I had a rosebud for you, but it is dead now."

"I went to Anvers. You looked for me a little, then?"

"Oh, all day long. For I was so afraid I had been ungrateful."

"That is very pretty of you. Women are never grateful, my dear, except when they are very ill-treated. Mercury, whom we were talking of, gave them, among other gifts, a dog's heart."

Bébée felt bewildered; she did not reason about it, but the idle, shallow, cynical tone, pained her by its levity and its unlikeness to the sweet, still, gray summer evening.

"Why are you in such a hurry?" he pursued. "The night is cool, and it is only seven o'clock. I will walk part of the way with you."

"I am in a hurry because I have Annémie's patterns to do," said Bébée, glad that he spoke of a thing that she knew how to answer. "You see, Annémie's hand shakes and her eyes are dim, and she pricks the pattern all awry and never perceives it; it would break her heart if one showed her so, but the Baës would not take them as they are; they are of no use at all. So I prick them out myself on fresh paper, and the Baës thinks it is all her doing, and pays her the same money, and she is quite content. And as I carry the patterns to and fro for her, because she cannot walk, it is easy to cheat her like that; and it is no harm to cheat *so*, you know." He was silent.

"You are a good little girl, Bébée, I can see," he said at last, with a graver sound in his voice. "And who is this Annémie for whom you do so much—an old woman, I suppose?"

"Oh, yes, quite old; incredibly old. Her man was drowned at sea sixty years ago, and she watches for his brig still, night and morning."

"The dog's heart. No doubt he beat her, and had a wife in fifty other ports."

"Oh, no," said Bébée, with a little cry, as though the word against the dead man hurt her. "She has told me so much of him. He was as good as good could be, and loved her so, and between the voyages they were so happy. Surely that must have been sixty years now, and she is so sorry still, and still will not believe that he was drowned."

He looked down on her with a smile that had a certain pity in it.

"Well, yes; there are women like that, I believe. But be very sure, my dear, he beat her. Of the two, one always holds the whip and uses it,—the other crouches."

"I do not understand," said Bébée.

"No—but you will."

"I will?—when?"

He smiled again.

"Oh—to-morrow, perhaps, or next year—or when Fate fancies."

"Or rather—when I choose," he thought to himself, and let his eyes rest with a certain pleasure on the little feet, that went beside him in the grass, and the pretty fair bosom that showed ever and again, as the frills of her linen bodice were blown back by the wind and her own quick motion.

Bébée looked also up at him; he was very handsome, and looked so to her, after the broad blunt characterless faces of the Walloon peasantry around her. He walked with an easy grace, he was clad in picture-like velvets, he had a beautiful poetic head, and eyes like deep brown waters, and a face like one of Jordaens' or Rembrandt's cavaliers in the galleries where she used to steal in of a Sunday, and look up at the paintings, and dream of what that world could be in which those people had lived.

"*You* are of the people of Rubes' country, are you not?" she asked him.

"Of what country, my dear?"

"Of the people that live in the gold frames," said Bébée, quite seriously. "In the galleries, you know. I know a charwoman that scrubs the floors of the Arenberg Palace, and she lets me in sometimes to look; and you are just like those great gentlemen in the gold frames, only you have not a hawk and a sword, and they always have. I used to wonder where they came from, for they are not like any of us one bit, and the charwoman—she is Lisa Dredel, and lives in the street of the Pot d'Etain—always said, 'Dear heart, they all belong to Rubes' land—we never see their like nowadays.' But *you* must come out of Rubes' land; at least, I think so, do you not?"

He caught her meaning; he knew that Rubes was the homely abbreviation of Rubens that all the Netherlanders used, and he guessed the idea that was reality to this little lonely fanciful mind.

"Perhaps I do," he answered her with a smile, for it was not worth his while to disabuse her thoughts of any imagination that glorified him to her. "Do you not want to see Rubes' world, little one? To see the gold and the grandeur, and the glitter of it all?—never to toil or get tired?—always to move in a pageant?—always to live like the hawks in the paintings you talk of, with silver bells hung round you, and a hood all sewn with pearls?"

"No," said Bébée, simply. "I should like to see it—just to see it, as one looks through a grating into the king's grape-houses here. But I should not like to live in it. I love my hut, and the starling, and the chickens, and what would the garden do without me?—and the children, and the old Annémie? I could not anyhow, anywhere, be any happier than I am. There is only one thing I wish."

"And what is that?"

"To know something; not to be so ignorant. Just look—I can read a little, it is true: my Hours, and the letters, and when Krebs brings in a newspaper I can read a little of it—not much. I know French well, because Antoine was French himself, and never did talk Flemish to me; and they being Netherlanders, cannot, of course, read the newspapers at all, and so think it very wonderful indeed in me. But what I want is to know things, to know all about what *was* before ever I was living. St. Gudule now—they say it was built hundreds of years before; and Rubes again—they say he was a painter-king in Antwerpen before the oldest oldest woman like Annémie ever began to count time. I am sure books tell you all those things, because I see the students coming and going with them; and when I saw once the millions of books in the Rue du Musée, I asked the keeper what use they were for, and he said, 'To make men wise, my dear.' But Gringoire Bac the cobbler, who was with me,—it was a fête day,—Bac, *he* said, 'Do not you believe that, Bébée; they only muddle folk's brains; for one book tells them one thing, and another book another, and so on, till they are dazed with all the contrary lying; and if you see a bookish man, be sure you see a very poor creature who could not hoe a patch, or kill a pig, or stitch an upper-leather, were it ever so.' But I do not believe that Bac said right. Did he?"

"I am not sure. On the whole, I think it is the truest remark on literature I have ever heard, and one that shows great judgment in Bac. Well?"

"Well—sometimes, you know," said Bébée, not understanding his answer, but pursuing her thoughts confidentially; "sometimes I talk like this to the neighbors, and they laugh at me. Because Mère Krebs says that when one knows how to spin and sweep and make bread and say one's prayers and milk a goat or a cow, it is all a woman wants to know this side of heaven. But for me, I cannot help it—when I look at those windows in the cathedral, or at those beautiful twisted little spires that are all over our Hôtel de Ville, I want to know who the men were that made them—what they did and thought—how they looked and spoke,—how they learned to shape stone into leaves and grasses like that—how they could imagine all those angel faces on the glass. When I go alone in the quite early morning or at night when it is still—sometimes in winter I have to stay till it is dark over the lace—I hear their feet come after me, and they whisper to me close, 'Look what beautiful things we have done, Bébée, and you all forget us quite. We did what never will die, but our names are as dead as the stones.' And then I am so sorry for them and ashamed. And I want to know more. Can you tell me?"

He looked at her earnestly; her eyes were shining, her cheeks were warm, her little mouth was tremulous with eagerness.

"Did any one ever speak to you in that way?" he asked her.

"No," she answered him. "It comes into my head of itself. Sometimes I think the cathedral angels put it there. For the angels must be tired, you know; always pointing to God and always seeing men turn away. I used to tell Antoine sometimes. But he used to shake his head and say that it was no use thinking; most likely St. Gudule and St. Michael had set the church down in the night all ready-made, why not? God made the trees, and they were more wonderful, he thought, for his part. And so perhaps they are.

but that is no answer. And I do *want* to know. I want some one who will tell me,—and if you come out of Rubes' country as I think, no doubt you know every thing, or remember it?"

He smiled.

"The free pass to Rubes' country lies in books, pretty one. Shall I give you some?—nay, lend them, I mean, since giving you are too willful to hear of without offense. You can read, you said?"

Bébée's eyes glowed as they lifted themselves to his.

"I can read—not very fast, but that would come with doing it more and more, I think, just as spinning does—one knots the thread and breaks it a million times before one learns to spin as fine as cobwebs. I have read the stories of St. Anne, and of St. Catherine, and of St. Luven fifty times, but they are all the books that Father Francis has; and no one else has any among us."

"Very well. You shall have books of mine. Easy ones first; and then those that are more serious. But what time will you have? You do so much; you are like a little golden bee."

Bébée laughed happily.

"Oh! give me the books and I will find the time. It is light so early now. That gives one so many hours. In winter one has so few one must lie in bed, because to buy a candle you know one cannot afford except of course, a taper now and then, as one's duty is, for our Lady or for the dead. And will you really, really, lend me books?"

"Really—I will. Yes. I will bring you one to the Grande Place to-morrow, or meet you on your road there with it. Do you know what poetry is, Bébée?"

"No."

"But your flowers talk to you?"

"Ah! always. But then no one else hears them ever but me; and so no one else ever believes."

"Well—poets are folks who hear the flowers talk as you do, and the trees, and the seas, and the beasts, and even the stones; but no one else ever hears these things, and so, when the poets write them out, the rest of the world say, 'That is very fine, no doubt, but only good for dreamers; it will bake no bread.' I will give you some poetry—for I think you care more about dreams than about bread."

"I do not know," said Bébée; and she did not know, for her dreams, like her youth and her innocence, and her simplicity, and her strength, were all unconscious of themselves, as such things must be to be pure and true at all.

Bébée had grown up straight, and clean, and fragrant, and joyous as one of her own carnations; but she knew herself no more than the carnation knows its color and its root.

"No, you do not know," said he, with a sort of pity; and thought within himself, was it worth while to let her know?

If she did not know, these vague aspirations and imaginations would drop off from her with the years of her early youth, as the lime-flowers drop downwards with the summer heats. She would forget them. They would linger a little in her head, and, perhaps, always wake at some sunset hour or some angelus chime, but not to trouble her. Only to make her cradle-song a little sadder and softer than most women's was. Unfed, they would sink away and bear no blossom.

She would grow into a simple, hardy, hard-working, God-fearing Flemish woman like the rest. She would marry, no doubt, some time, and rear her children honestly and well; and sit in the market-stall every day, and spin and sew, and dig and wash, and sweep, and brave bad weather, and be content with poor food to the end of her harmless and laborious days—poor little Bébée!

He saw her so clearly as she would be—if he let her alone.

A little taller, a little broader, a little browner, less sweet of voice, less soft of skin, less flower-like in face; having learned to think only as her neighbors thought, of price of wood and cost of bread; laboring cheerily but hardly from daybreak to nightfall to fill hungry mouths; forgetting all things except the little curly-heads clustered round her soup-pot, and the year-old lips sucking at her breasts.

A blameless life, an eventless life, a life as clear as the dew-drop, and as colorless; a life opening, passing, ending in the little green wooded lane, by the bit of water where the swans made their nests under the willows; a life like the life of millions, a little purer, a little brighter, a little more tender, perhaps, than those lives usually are, but otherwise as like them as one ear of barley is like another as it rises from the soil, and blows in the wind, and turns brown in the strong summer sun, and then goes down to the sod again under the sickle.

He saw her just as she would be—if he let her alone.

But should he leave her alone?

He cared nothing; only her eyes had such a pretty, frank, innocent look like a bird's in them, and she had been so brave and bold with him about those silken stockings; and this little ignorant, dreamful mind of hers was so like a blush rosebud, which looks so close-shut, and so sweet-smelling, and so tempting fold within fold, that a child will pull it open, forgetful that he will spoil it forever from being a full-grown rose, and that he will let the dust, and the sun, and the bee into its tender bosom—and men are true children, and women are their rosebuds.

Thinking only of keeping well with this strange and beautiful wayfarer from that unknown paradise of Rubes' country, Bébée lifted up the vine-leaves of her basket.

"I took a flower for you to-day, but it is dead. Look—to-morrow, if you will be there, you shall have the best in all the garden."

"You wish to see me again then?" he asked her. Bébée looked at him with troubled eyes, but with a sweet frank faith that had no hesitation in it.

"Yes! you are not like anything I ever knew, and if you will only help me to learn a little. Sometimes I think I am not stupid, only ignorant—but I cannot be sure unless I try."

He smiled; he was listlessly amused; the day before he had tempted the child merely because she was pretty, and to tempt her in that way seemed the natural course of things, but now there was something in her that touched him differently; the end would be the same, but he would change the means.

The sun had set. There was a low, dull red glow still on the far edge of the plains—that was all. In the distant cottages little lights were twinkling. The path grew dark.

"I will go away and let her alone," he thought. "Poor little soul! it would give itself lavishly, it would never be bought. I will let it alone; the mind will go to sleep and the body will keep healthy and strong and pure, as people call it. It would be a pity to play with both a day, and then throw them away as the boy threw the pear-blossom. She is a little clod of earth that has field-flowers growing in it. I will let her alone, the flowers under the plow in due course will die, and she will be content among the other clods,—if I let her alone."

At that moment there went across the dark fields,

against the dusky red sky, a young man with a pile of brushwood on his back, and a hatchet in his hand.

"You are late, Bébée," he called to her in Flemish, and scowled at the stranger by her side.

"A good-looking lad—who is it?" said her companion.

"That is Jeannot, the son of old Sophie," she answered him. "He is so good—oh, so good, you cannot think; he keeps his mother and three little sisters, and works so very, very hard in the forest, and yet he often finds time to dig my garden for me, and he chops all my wood in winter."

They had come to where the road goes up by the king's summer-palace. They were under great hanging beeches and limes. There was a high gray wall, and over it the blossoming fruit-boughs hung. In a ditch full of long grass little kids bleated by their mothers. Away on the left went the green fields of colza, and beetroot, and trefoil, with big forest-trees here and there in their midst, and, against the blue low line of the far horizon, red mill-sails, and gray church spires; dreamy plaintive bells far away somewhere were ringing the sad, Flemish carillon.

He paused and looked at her.

"I must bid you good-night, Bébée—you are near your home now."

She paused too and looked at him.

"But I shall see you to-morrow?"

There was the wistful, eager, anxious unconsciousness of appeal as when the night before she had asked him if he were angry.

He hesitated a moment. If he said no, and went away out of the city wherever his listless and changeful whim called him, he knew how it would be with her; he knew what her life would be as surely as he knew the peach would come out of the peach-flower rosy on the wall there: life in the little hut; among the neighbors; sleepy and safe and soulless;—if he let her alone.

If he stayed and saw her on the morrow he knew, too, the end as surely as he knew that the branch of white pear-blossom which in carelessness he had knocked down with a stone on the grass yonder, would fade in the night and would never bring forth its sweet, simple fruit in the sunshine.

To leave the peach-flower to come to maturity and be plucked by a peasant—or to pull down the pear-blossom and rifle the buds?

Carelessly and languidly he balanced the question with himself, whilst Bébée, forgetful of the lace patterns and the flight of the hours, stood looking at him with anxious and pleading eyes, thinking only—was he angry again, or would he really bring her the books and make her wise, and let her know the stories of the past?

"Shall I see you to-morrow?" she said wistfully.

Should she?—if he left the peach-blossom safe on the wall, Jeannot the woodcutter would come by-and-by and gather the fruit.

If he left the clod of earth in its pasture with all its daisies untouched, this black-browed young peasant would cut it round with his hatchet and carry it to his wicker cage, that the homely brown lark of his love might sing to it some stupid wood note under a cottage eave.

The sight of the strong young forester going over the darkened fields against the dull red skies was as a feather that suffices to sway to one side a balance that hangs on a hair.

He had been inclined to leave her alone when he saw in his fancy the clean, simple, mindless, honest life that her fanciful girlhood would settle down into as time should go on. But when in the figure of the woodman there was painted visibly on the dusky sky that end for her which he had foreseen, he was not indifferent to it; he resented it; he was stirred to a vague desire to render it impossible.

If Jeannot had not gone by across the fields he would have left her and let her alone from that night thenceforwards; as it was,—

"Good-night, Bébée," he said to her. "To-morrow I will finish the Broodhuis and bring you your first book. Do not dream too much, or you will prick your lace patterns all awry. Good-night, pretty one."

Then he turned and went back through the green dim lanes to the city.

Bébée stood a moment looking after him, with a happy smile; then she picked up the fallen peach-bough, and ran home as fast as her feet would take her.

That night she worked very late watering her flowers, and trimming them, and then ironing out a little clean white cap for the morrow; and then sitting down under the open lattice to prick out all old Annémie's designs by the strong light of the full moon that flooded her hut with its radiance.

But she sang all the time she worked, and the gay, pretty, wordless songs floated across the water and across the fields, and woke some old people in their beds as they lay with their windows open, and they turned and crossed themselves, and said, "Dear heart!—this is the Eve of the Ascension, and the angels are so near we hear them."

But it was no angel; only the thing that is nearer heaven than anything else—a little human heart that is happy and innocent.

Bébée had only one sorrow that night. The peach-blossoms were all dead—and no care could call them back even for an hour's blooming.

"He did not think when he struck them down," she said to herself, regretfully.

CHAPTER VIII.

"CAN I do any work for you, Bébée?" said black Jeannot in the daybreak, pushing her gate open timidly with one hand.

"There is none to do, Jeannot. They want so little in this time of the year—the flowers," said she, lifting her head from the sweet-peas she was tying up to their sticks.

The woodman did not answer; he leaned over the half-open wicket, and swayed it backwards and forwards under his bare arm. He was a good, harmless, gentle fellow, swarthy as charcoal and simple as a child, and quite ignorant; having spent all his days in the great Soignies forests making fagots when he was a little lad, and hewing down trees or burning charcoal as he grew to manhood.

"Who was that seigneur with you last night, Bébée?" he asked, after a long silence, watching her as she moved.

Bébée's eyes grew very soft, but they looked up frankly.

"I am not sure—I think he is a painter—a great painter-prince, I mean—as Rubes was in Antwerpen; he wanted roses the night before last in the cathedral."

"But he was walking with you?"

"He was in the lane as I came home last night —yes."

"What does he give you for your roses?"

"Oh—he pays me well. How is your mother this day, Jeannot?"

"You do not like to talk of him?"

"Why should you want to talk of him?—he is nothing to you."

"Did you really see him only two days ago, Bébée?"

"Oh, Jeannot!—did I ever tell a falsehood?—you would not say that to one of your little sisters."

The forester swayed the gate to and fro drearily under his folded arms.

Bébée, not regarding him, cut her flowers, and filled her baskets, and did her other work, and set a ladder against the hut and climbed on its low roof to seek for eggs, the hens having green tastes sometimes for the rushes and lichens of its thatch. She found two eggs, which she promised herself to take to Annémie, and looking round as she sat on the edge of the roof, with one foot on the highest rung of the ladder, saw that Jeannot was still at the gate.

"You will be late in the forest, Jeannot," she cried to him. "It is such a long, long way in and out. Why do you look so sulky? and you are kicking the wicket to pieces."

"I do not like you to talk with strangers," said Jeannot, sullenly and sadly.

Bébée laughed as she sat on the edge of the thatch, and looked at the shining gray skies of the early day, and the dew-wet garden, and the green fields beyond, with happy eyes that made the familiar scene transfigured to her.

"Oh, Jeannot, what nonsense! As if I do not talk to a million strangers every summer! as if I could ever sell a flower if I did not! You are cross this morning—that is what it is."

"Do you know the man's name?" said Jeannot, suddenly.

Bébée felt her cheeks grow warm as with some noonday heat of sunshine. She thought it was with anger against blundering Jeannot's curiosity.

"No! and what would his name be to us, if I did know it? I cannot ask people's names because they buy my roses."

"As if it were only roses!——"

There was the length of the garden between them, and Bébée did not hear as she sat on the edge of her roof with that light dreamful enjoyment of air and sky and coolness, and all the beauty of the dawning day, which the sweet vague sense of a personal happiness will bring with it to the dullest and the coldest.

"You are cross, Jeannot, that is what it is," she said, after awhile. "You should not be cross; you are too big and strong and good. Go in and get my bowl of bread and milk for me, and hand it to me up here. It is so pleasant. It is as nice as being perched on an apple-tree."

Jeannot went in obediently and handed up her breakfast to her, looking at her with shy, worshiping eyes. But his face was overcast, and he sighed heavily as he took up his hatchet and turned away; for he was the sole support of his mother and sisters, and if he did not do his work in Soignies they would starve at home.

"You will be seeing that stranger again?" he asked her.

"Yes!" she answered, with a glad triumph in her eyes; not thinking at all of him as she spoke. "You ought to go, Jeannot, now; you are so late. I will come and see your mother to-morrow. And do not be cross, you dear big Jeannot. Days are too short to snip them up into little bits by bad temper; it is only a stupid sheep-shearer that spoils the fleece by snapping at it sharp and hard—that is what Father Francis says."

Bébée having delivered her little piece of wisdom, broke her bread into her milk and ate it, lifting her face to the fresh wind and tossing crumbs to the wheeling swallows, and watching the rose-bushes nod and toss below in the breeze, and thinking vaguely how happy a thing it was to live.

Jeannot looked up at her, then went on his slow sad way through the wet lavender-shrubs and the opening buds of the lilies.

"You will only think of that stranger, Bébée, never of any of us—never again," he said; and wearily opened the little gate and went through it, and down the daybreak stillness of the lane. It was a foolish thing to say; but when were lovers ever wise?

Bébée did not heed; she did not understand herself or him; she only knew that she was happy; when one knows that, one does not want to seek much further.

She sat on the thatch and took her bread and milk in the gray clear air, with the swallows circling above her head, and one or two of them even resting a second on the edge of the bowl to peck at the food from the big wooden spoon; they had known her all the sixteen summers of her life, and were her playfellows, only they would never tell her anything of what they saw in winter over the seas. That was her only quarrel with them. Swallows do not tell their secrets. They have the weird of Procne on them all.

The sun came and touched the lichens of the roof into gold.

Bébée smiled at it gayly as it rose above the tops of the trees, and shone on all the little villages scattered over the plains.

"Ah, dear Sun!" she cried to it. "I am going to be wise. I am going into great Rubes' country. I am going to hear of the Past and the Future. I am going to listen to what the Poets say. The swallows never would tell me anything; but now I shall know as much as they know. Are you not glad for me, O Sun?"

The Sun came over the trees, and heard and said nothing. If he had answered at all he must have said,—

"The only time when a human soul is either wise or happy, is in that one single moment when the hour of my own shining or of the moon's beaming seems to that single soul to be past and present and future, to be at once the creation and the end of all things. Faust knew that; so will you."

But the Sun shone on and held his peace. He sees all things ripen and fall. He can wait. He knows the end. It is always the same.

He brings the fruit out of the peach-flower, and rounds it and touches it into ruddiest rose and softest gold; but the sun knows well that the peach must drop—whether into the basket to be eaten by kings, or on to the turf to be eaten by ants. What matter which very much after all?

The Sun is not a cynic; he is only wise because he is Life and he is Death, the creator and the corrupter of all things.

CHAPTER IX.

BUT Bébée, who only saw in the sun the sign of daily work, the brightness of the face of the world, the friend of the flowers, the harvest-man of the poor, the playmate of the birds and butterflies, the kindly light that the waking birds and the ringing carillon welcomed—Bébée, who was not at all afraid of him, smiled at his rays and saw in them only fairest promise of a cloudless midsummer day as she gave her last crumb to the swallows, dropped down off the thatch, and busied herself in making bread that Mère Krebs would bake for her, until it was time to cut her flowers and go down into the town.

When her loaves were made and she had run over with them to the mill-house and back again, she attired herself with more heed than usual, and ran to look at her own face in the mirror of the deep well-water—other glass she had none.

She was used to hear herself called pretty; but she had never thought about it at all till now. The people loved her; she had always believed that they had only said it as a sort of kindness, as they said, "God keep you." But now—

"He told me I was like a flower," she thought to herself, and hung over the well to see. She did not know very well what he had meant; but the sentence stirred in her heart as a little bird under tremulous leaves.

She waited ten minutes full, leaning and looking down, while her eyes, that were like the blue iris, smiled back to her from the brown depths below. Then she went and kneeled down before the old shrine in the wall of the garden.

"Dear and holy Mother of Jesus, I do thank you that you made me a little good to look at," she said, softly. "Keep me as you keep the flowers, and let my face be always fair, because it is a pleasure to *be* a pleasure. Ah, dear Mother, I say it so badly, and it sounds so vain, I know. But I do not think you will be angry, will you? And I am going to try to be wise."

Then she murmured an ave or two, to be in form as it were, and then rose and ran along the lanes with her baskets, and brushed the dew lightly over her bare feet, and sang a little Flemish song for very joyousness, as the birds sing in the apple-bough.

She got the money for Annémie and took it to her with fresh patterns to prick, and the new-laid eggs.

"I wonder what he meant by a dog's heart?" she thought to herself, as she left the old woman sitting by the hole in the roof pricking out the parchment in all faith that she earned her money, and looking every now and then through the forests of masts for the brig with the hank of flax flying,—the brig that had foundered fifty long years before in the northern seas, and in the days of her youth.

"What is the dog's heart?" thought Bébée; she had seen a dog she knew—a dog who all his life long had dragged heavy loads under brutal stripes along the streets of Brussels—stretch himself on the grave of his taskmaster and refuse to eat, and persist in lying there until he died, though he had no memory except of stripes, and no tie to the dead except pain and sorrow. Was it a heart like this that he meant?

"Was her sailor, indeed, so good to her?" she asked an old gossip of Annémie's, as she went down the stairs.

The old soul stopped to think with difficulty of such a far-off time, and resting her brass flagon of milk on the steep step.

"Eh, no; not that I ever saw," she answered at length. "He was fond of her—very fond; but he was a willful one, and he beat her sometimes when he got tired of being on land. But women must not mind that, you know, my dear, if only a man's heart is right. Things fret them, and then they belabor what they love best; it is a way they have.

"But she speaks of him as of an angel nearly!" said Bébée, bewildered.

The old woman took up her flagon, with a smile flitting across her wintry face.

"Ay, dear; when the frost kills your brave rosebush, root and bud, do you think of the thorns that pricked you, or only of the fair, sweet-smelling things that flowered all your summer?"

Bébée went away thoughtfully out of the old crazy water-washed house by the quay; life seemed growing very strange and intricate and knotted about her, like the threads of lace that a bad fairy has entangled in the night.

CHAPTER X.

HER stranger from Rubes' land was a great man in a certain world. He had become great when young, which is perhaps a misfortune. It indisposes men to be great at their maturity. He was famous at twenty, by a picture hectic in color, perfect in drawing, that made Paris at his feet. He became more famous by verses, by plays, by political follies, and by social successes. He was faithful, however, to his first love in art. He was a great painter, and year by year proved afresh the cunning of his hand. Purists said his pictures had no soul in them. It was not wonderful if they had none. He always painted soulless vice; indeed, he saw very little else.

One year he had some political trouble. He wrote a witty pamphlet that hurt where it was perilous to aim. He laughed and crossed the border, riding into the green Ardennes one sunny evening. He had a name of some power and sufficient wealth; he did not fear long exile. Meanwhile he told himself he would go and look at Scheffer's Gretchen.

The King of Thule is better; but people talk most of the Gretchen. He had never seen either.

He went in leisurely, traveling up the bright Meuse River, and across the monotony of the plains, then green with wheat a foot high, and musical with the many bells of the Easter kermesses in the quaint old-world villages.

There was something so novel, so sleepy, so harmless, so mediæval, in the Flemish life, that it soothed him. He had been swimming all his life in salt sea-fed rapids; this sluggish, dull canal-water, mirroring between its rushes a life that had scarcely changed for centuries, had a charm for him.

He stayed awhile in Antwerpen. The town is ugly and beautiful; it is like a dull quaint grès de Flandre jug, that has precious stones set inside its rim. It is a burgher ledger of bales and barrels, of sale and barter, of loss and gain; but in the heart of it there are illuminated leaves of missal vellum, all gold and color, and monkish story and heroic ballad, that could only have been executed in the days when Art was a religion.

He gazed himself into an homage of Rubens, whom before he had slighted, never having known (for, unless you have seen Antwerp, it is as absurd to say that you have seen Rubens, as it is to think that you have seen Murillo out of Seville, or Raffaelle out of Rome); and he studied the Gretchen carefully, delicately, sympathetically, for he loved Scheffer; but though he tried, he failed to care for her.

"She is only a peasant; she is not a poem," he said to himself; "I will paint a Gretchen for the Salon of next year."

But it was hard for him to portray a Gretchen. All his pictures were Phryne—Phryne in triumph, in ruin, in a palace, in a poor-house, on a bed of roses, on a hospital mattress; Phryne laughing with a belt of jewels about her supple waist; Phryne lying with the stones of the dead-house under her naked limbs—but always Phryne. Phryne, who living had death in her smile; Phryne, who lifeless had blank despair on her face; Phryne, a thing that lived furiously every second of her days, but Phryne a thing that once being dead was carrion that never could live again.

Phryne has many painters in this school, as many as Catherine and Cecilia had in the schools of the Renaissance, and he was chief amidst them.

How could he paint Gretchen if the pure Scheffer missed? Not even if, like the artist monks of old, he steeped his brushes all Lent through in holy water.

And in holy water he did not believe.

One evening, having left Antwerpen ringing its innumerable bells over the grave of its dead Art, he leaned out of the casement of an absent friend's old palace in the Brabant street that is named after Mary of Burgundy; an old casement crusted with quaint carvings, and gilded round in Spanish fashion, with many gargoyles and griffins, and illegible scutcheons.

Leaning there, wondering with himself whether he would wait awhile and paint quietly in this dim street, haunted with the shades of Memling and Maes, and Otto Veneris and Philip de Champagne, or whether he would go into the East and seek new types, and lie under the red Egyptian heavens and create a true Cleopatra, which no man has ever done yet—a young Cleopatra, ankle-deep in roses and fresh from Cæsar's kisses—leaning there, he saw a little peasant go by below, with two little white feet in two wooden shoes, and a face that had the pure and simple radiance of a flower.

"There is my Gretchen," he thought to himself, and went down and followed her into the cathedral. If he could get what was in her face, he would get what Scheffer could not.

A little later, walking by her in the green lanes, he meditated, "It is the face of Gretchen, but not the soul—the Red Mouse has never passed this child's lips. Nevertheless——"

"Nevertheless——" he said to himself, and smiled.

For he, the painter all his life long of Phryne living and of Phryne dead, believed that every daughter of Eve either vomits the Red Mouse or swallows it.

It makes so little difference which,—either way the Red Mouse has been there.

And yet, strolling there in the dusky red of the evening towards this little rush-covered hut, he forgot the Red Mouse, and began vague'y to see that there are creatures of his mother's sex from whom the beast of the Brocken slinks away.

But he still said to himself, "Nevertheless."

"Nevertheless,"—for he knew well that when the steel cuts the silk, when the hound hunts the fawn, when the snake wooes the bird, when the king covets the vineyard, there is only one end possible at any time. It is the strong against the weak, the fierce against the feeble, the subtle against the simple, the master against the slave; there is no equality in the contest and no justice—it is merely inevitable, and the issue of it is written.

CHAPTER XI.

THE next day she had her promised book hidden under the vine-leaves of her empty basket as she went homeward, and though she had not seen him very long or spoken to him very much, she was happy.

The golden gates of knowledge had just opened to her; she saw a faint, far-off glimpse of the Hesperides gardens within; of the dragon she had never heard, and had no fear.

"Might I know your name?" she had asked him wistfully, as she had given him the rosebud, and taken the volume in return that day.

"They call me Flamen."

"It is your name?"

"Yes, for the world. You must call me Victor, as other women do. Why do you want my name?"

"Jeannot asked it of me."

"Oh, Jeannot asked it, did he?"

"Yes; besides," said Bébée, with her eyes very soft and very serious, and her happy voice hushed, "besides, I want to pray for you of course, every day; and if I do not know your name, how can I make Our Lady rightly understand? The flowers know you without a name, but she might not, because so very many are always beseeching her, and you see she has all the world to look after."

He had looked at her with a curious look, and had bade her farewell, and let her go home alone that night.

Her work was quickly done, and by the light of the moon she spread her book on her lap in the porch of the hut and began her new delight.

The children had come and pulled at her skirts and begged her to play. But Bébée had shaken her head.

"I am going to learn to be very wise, dear," she told them; "I shall not have time to dance or to play."

"But people are not merry when they are wise, Bébée," said Franz, the biggest boy.

"Perhaps not," said Bébée; "but one cannot be everything, you know, Franz."

"But surely, you would rather be merry than anything else?"

"I think there is something better, Franz. I am not sure; I want to find out; I will tell you when I know."

"Who has put that into your head, Bébée?"

"The angels in the cathedral," she told them; and the children were awed and left her, and went away to play blind-man's-buff by themselves, on the grass by the swan's water.

"But for all that the angels have said it," said Franz to his sisters, "I cannot see what good it will be to her to be wise, if she will not care any longer afterwards for almond ginger-bread, and currant-cake."

It was the little tale of "Paul and Virginia" that he had given her to begin her studies with; but it was a grand copy, full of beautiful drawings nearly at every page.

It was hard work for her to read at first, but the drawings enticed and helped her, and she soon sank breathlessly into the charm of the story. Many words she did not know; many passages were beyond her comprehension; she was absolutely ignorant, and had nothing but the force of her own fancy to aid her.

But though stumbling at every step, as a lame child through a flowery hillside in summer, she was happy as the child would be, because of the sweet, strange air that was blowing about her, and the blossoms that she could gather into her hand, so rare, so wonderful, and yet withal so familiar, because they *were* blossoms.

With her fingers buried in her curls, with her book on her knee, with the moonrays white and strong on the page, Bébée sat entranced as the hours went by; the children's play shouts died away; the babble of the gossip at the house doors ceased; people went by and called good-night to her; the little huts shut up one by one, like the white and purple convolvulus cups in the hedges.

Bébée did not stir, nor did she hear them; she was deaf even to the singing of the nightingales in the willows, where she sat in her little dark porch, with the ivy dropping from the thatch above, and the wet garden-ways beyond her.

A heavy step came tramping down the lane. A voice called to her,—

"What are you doing, Bébée, there this time of the night? It is on the strike of twelve."

She started as if she were doing some evil thing, and stretched her arms out, and looked around with blinded, wondering eyes, as if she had been rudely wakened from her sleep.

"What are you doing up so late?" asked Jeannot; he was coming from the forest in the dead of night to bring food for his family; he lost his sleep thus often, but he never thought that he did anything except his duty in those long, dark, tiring tramps to and fro between Soignies and Laeken.

Bébée shut her book and smiled with dreaming eyes, that saw him not at all.

"I was reading —— and, Jeannot, his name is Flamen for the world—but I may call him Victor."

"What do I care for his name?"

"You asked it this morning."

"More fool I. Why do you read? Reading is not for poor folk like you and me."

Bébée smiled up at the white clear moon that sailed above the woods.

She was not awake out of her dream. She only dimly heard the words he spoke.

"You are a little peasant," said Jeannot roughly,

as he paused at the gate. "It is all you can do to get your bread. You have no one to stand between you and hunger. How will it be with you when the slug gets your roses, and the snail your carnations, and your hens die of damp, and your lace is all wove awry, because your head runs on reading and folly, and you are spoilt for all simple pleasures and for all honest work?"

She smiled, still looking up at the moon, with the dropping ivy touching her hair.

"You are cross, dear Jeannot. Good-night."

A moment afterwards the little rickety door was shut, and the rusty bolt drawn within it; Jeannot stood in the cool summer night all alone, and knew how stupid he had been in his wrath.

He leaned on the gate a minute; then crossed the garden as softly as his wooden shoes would let him. He tapped gently on the shutter of the lattice.

"Bébée—Bébée—just listen. I spoke roughly, dear—I know I have no right. I am sorry. Will you be friends with me again?—do be friends again."

She opened the shutter a little way, so that he could see her pretty mouth speaking.

"Oh, Jeannot, what does it matter? Yes, we are friends—we will always be friends, of course—only you do not know. Good-night."

He went away with a heavy heart and a long-drawn step. He would have preferred that she should have been angry with him.

Bébée, left alone, let the clothes drop off her

pretty round shoulders and her rosy limbs, and shook out her coils of hair, and kissed the book, and laid it under her head, and went to sleep with a smile on her face.

Only, as she slept, her fingers moved as if she were counting her beads, and her lips murmured.

"Oh, dear Holy Mother, you have so much to think of—yes, I know—all the poor, and all the little children. But take care of *him;* he is called Flamen, and he lives in the street of Mary of Burgundy; you cannot miss him; and if you will look for him always, and have a heed that the angels never leave him, I will give you my great cactus flower — my only one — on your Feast of Roses this very year. Oh, dear Mother, you will not forget!"

CHAPTER XII.

ÉBÉE was a dreamer in her way, and aspired to be a scholar too. But all the same, she was not a little fool.

She had been reared in hardy, simple, honest ways of living, and would have thought it as shameful as a theft to have owed her bread to other folk.

So, though she had a wakeful, restless night, full of strange phantasies, none the less was she out in her garden by daybreak; none the less did she sweep out her floor and make her mash for the fowls, and wash out her bit of linen and hang it to dry on a line among the tall, flaunting hollyhocks that were so proud of themselves because they reached to the roof.

"What do you want with books, Bébée?" said Reine, the sabot-maker's wife, across the privet hedge, as she also hung out her linen. "Franz told me you were reading last night. It is the silver buckles have done that: one mischief always begets another."

"Where is the mischief, good Reine?" said Bébée, who was always prettily behaved with her elders, though, when pushed to it, she could hold her own.

"The mischief will be in discontent," said the sabot-maker's wife. "People live on their own little patch, and think it is the world; that is as it should be—everybody within his own, like a nut in its shell. But when you get reading, you hear of a swarm of things you never saw, and you fret because you cannot see them, and you dream, and dream, and a hole is burnt in your soup-pot, and your dough is as heavy as lead. You are like bees that leave their own clover-fields to buzz themselves dead against the glass of a hot-house."

Bébée smiled, reaching to spread out her linen. But she said nothing.

"What good is it talking to them?" she thought; "they do not know."

Already the neighbors and friends of her infancy seemed so far, far away; creatures of a distant world, that she had long left; it was no use talking, they never would understand.

"Antoine should never have taught you your letters," said Reine, groaning under the great blue shirts she was hanging on high among the leaves. "I told him so at the time. I said, 'The child is a good child, and spins, and sews, and sweeps, rare and fine for her age—why go and spoil her?' But he was always headstrong. Not a child of mine knows a letter,—the saints be praised! nor a word of any tongue but our own good Flemish. You should have been brought up the same. You would have come to no trouble then."

"I am in no trouble, dear Reine," said Bébée, scattering the potato-peels to the clacking poultry, and she smiled into the faces of the golden oxlips that nodded to her back again in sunshiny sympathy.

"Not yet," said Reine, hanging her last shirt.

But Bébée was not hearing; she was calling the chickens, and telling the oxlips how pretty they looked in the borders; and in her heart she was counting the minutes till the old Dutch cuckoo-clock at Mère Krebs's—the only clock in the lane—should crow out the hour at which she went down to the city.

She loved the hut, the birds, the flowers; but they were little to her now compared with the dark golden picturesque square, the changing crowds, the frowning roofs, the gray stones, and the delight of watching through the shifting colors and shadows of the throngs for one face and for one smile.

"He is sure to be there," she thought, and started half an hour earlier than was her wont. She wanted to tell him all her rapture in the book—no one else could understand.

But all the day through he never came.

Bébée sat with a sick heart and a parched little throat, selling her flowers and straining her eyes through the tumult of the square.

The whole day went by, and there was no sign of him.

The flowers had sold well: it was a feast-day; her pouch was full of pence—what was that to her?

She went and prayed in the cathedral, but it seemed cold, and desolate, and empty; even the storied windows seemed dark.

"Perhaps he is gone out of the city," she thought; and a terror fell on her that frightened her, it was so unlike any fear that she had ever known—even the fear when she had seen death on old Antoine's face had been nothing like this.

Going home through the streets, she passed the café of the Trois Frères that looks out on the trees of the park, and that has flowers in its balconies, and pleasant windows that stand open to let the sounds of the soldiers' music enter. She saw him in one of the windows. There were amber and scarlet and black; silks and satins and velvets. There was a fan painted and jeweled. There were women's faces. There was a heap of purple fruit, and glittering sweetmeats. He laughed there. His beautiful Murillo head was dark against the white and gold within.

Bébée looked up—paused a second,—then went onward, with a thorn in her heart.

He had not seen her.

"It is natural, of course—he has his world—he does not think often of me—there is no reason why he should be as good as he is," she said to herself as she went slowly over the stones.

She had the dog's soul — only she did not know it.

But the tears fell down her cheeks, as she walked.

It looked so bright in there, so gay, with the sound of the music coming in through the trees, and those women — she had seen such women before; sometimes in the winter nights, going home from the lace-work, she had stopped at the doors of the palaces, or of the opera-house, when the carriages were setting down their brilliant burdens; and sometimes on the great feast-days she had seen the people of the court going out to some gala at the theatre, or some great review of troops, or some ceremonial of foreign sovereigns; but she had never thought about them before; she had never wondered whether velvet was better to wear than woolen serge, or diamonds lighter on the head than a little cap of linen.

But now—

Those women seemed to her so dazzlingly, so wondrously, so superhumanly beautiful; they seemed like some of those new dahlia flowers, rose and purple and gold, that outblazed the sun on the south border of her little garden, and blanched all the soft color out of the homely roses, and pimpernels, and sweet-williams, and double-stocks, that had bloomed there ever since the days of Waterloo.

But, the dahlias had no scent—and Bébée wondered if these women had any heart in them—they looked all laughter, and glitter, and vanity. To the child, whose dreams of womanhood were evolved from the face of the Mary of the Assumption, of the Susannah of Mieris, and of that Angel in the blue coif whose face has a light as of the sun,—to her who had dreamed her way into vague perceptions of her own sex's maidenhood and maternity by help of those great pictures which had been before her sight from infancy, there was some taint, some artifice, some want, some harshness in these jeweled women; she could not have reasoned about it, but she felt it, as she felt that the grand dahlias missed a flower's divinity, being scentless.

She was a little bit of wild thyme herself; hardy, fragrant, clean, tender, flowering by the wayside, full of honey, though only nourished on the turf and the stones—these gaudy, brilliant, ruby-bright, scarlet-mantled dahlias hurt her with a dim sense of pain and shame.

Fasting, next day at sunrise she confessed to Father Francis:

"I saw beautiful rich women, and I envied them; and I could not pray to Mary last night for thinking of them—for I hated them so much."

But she did not say,—

"I hated them because they were with him."

Out of the purest little soul, Love entering drives forth Candor.

"That is not like you at all, Bébée," said the good old man, as she knelt at his feet on the bricks of his little bare study, where all the books he ever spelt out were treatises on the art of bee-keeping

"My dear, you never were covetous at all, nor did you ever seem to care for the things of the world. I wish Jehan had not given you those silver buckles; I think they have set your little soul on vanities."

"It is not the buckles; I am not covetous," said Bébée; and then her face grew warm. She did not know why, and she did not hear the rest of Father Francis's admonitions.

CHAPTER XIII.

BUT the next noon-time brought him to the market-stall, and the next also, and so the summer days slipped away, and Bébée was quite happy if she saw him in the morning-time, to give him a fresh rose, or at evening by the gates, or under the beech-trees, when he brought her a new book, and sauntered awhile up the green lane beside her.

An innocent, unconscious love like Bébée's wants so little food to make it all content. Such mere trifles are beautiful and sweet to it. Such slender stray gleams of light suffice to make a broad, bright golden noon of perfect joy around it.

All the delirium, and fever, and desire, and despair, that are in maturer passion, are far away from it: far as is the flash of the meteor across sultry skies from the blue forget-me-not down in the brown meadow brook.

It was very wonderful to Bébée that he, this stranger from Rubes' Fairy-land, could come at all to keep pace with her little clattering wooden shoes over the dust and the grass in the dim twilight-time. The days went by in a trance of sweet amaze, and she kept count of the hours no more by the cuckoo-clock of the millhouse, or the deep chimes of the Brussels belfries; but only by such moments as brought her a word from his lips, or even a glimpse of him from afar, across the crowded square.

She sat up half the nights reading the books he gave her, studying the long cruel polysyllables, and spelling slowly through the phrases that seemed to her so cramped and tangled, and which yet were a pleasure to unravel for sake of the thought they held.

For Bébée, ignorant little simple soul that she was, had a mind in her that was eager, observant, quick to acquire, skillful to retain; and it would happen in certain times that Flamen, speaking to her of the things which he gave to her to read, would think to himself that this child had more wisdom than was often to be found in schools.

Meanwhile he pondered various studies in various stages of a Gretchen, and made love to Bébée —made love at least by his eyes and by his voice, not hurrying his pleasant task, but hovering about her softly, and mindful not to scare her, as a man will gently lower his hand over a poised butterfly that he seeks to kill, and which one single movement, a thought too quick, may scare away to safety.

Bébée knew where he lived in the street of Mary of Burgundy; in an old palace that belonged to a great Flemish noble, who never dwelt there himself; but to ask anything about him—why he was there? what his rank was? why he stayed in the city at all? was a sort of treason that never entered her thoughts.

Psyche, if she had been as simple and loyal as Bébée was, would never have lighted her own candle; but even Psyche would not have borrowed any one else's lamp to lighten the love darkness.

To Bébée he was sacred, unapproachable, unquestionable; he was a wonderful, perfect happiness that had fallen into her life; he was a gift of God, as the sun was.

She took his going and coming as she took that of the sun, never dreaming of reproaching his absence, never dreaming of asking if in the empty night he shone on any other worlds than hers.

It was hardly so much a faith with her as an instinct; faith must reason ere it know itself to be faith. Bébée never reasoned any more than her roses did.

The good folks in the market-place watched her a little anxiously: they thought ill of that little moss-rose that every day found its way to one wearer only; but after all they did not see much, and the neighbors nothing at all. For he never went home to her, nor with her, and most of the time that he spent with Bébée was in the quiet evening shadows, as she went up with her empty basket through the deserted country roads.

Bébée was all day long in the city, indeed, as other girls were, but with her it had always been different. Antoine had always been with her up to the day of his death; and after his death she had sat in the same place, surrounded by the people she had known from infancy, and an insult to her would have been answered by a stroke from the cobbler's strap or from the tinker's hammer. There was one girl only who ever tried to do her any harm—a good-looking, stout wench, who stood at the corner of the Montagne de la Cour with a stall of fruit in the summer-time, and in winter-time drove a milk-cart over the snow. This girl would get at her sometimes, and talk of the students, and tell her how good it was to get out of the town on a holiday, and go to any one of the villages where there was Kermesse and dance, and drink the little blue wine, and have trinkets bought for one, and come home in the moonlight in a char-à-banc, with the horns sounding, and the lads singing, and the ribbons flying from the old horse's ears.

"She is such a little close sly thing!" thought the fruit-girl, sulkily. To vice, innocence must always seem only a superior kind of chicanery.

"We dance almost every evening, the children and I," Bébée had answered when urged fifty times by this girl to go to fairs, and balls at the wine-shops. "That does just as well. And I have seen Kermesse once at Malines—it was beautiful. I went with Mère Dax, but it cost a great deal I know, though she did not let me pay."

"You little fool!" the fruit-girl would say, and grin, and eat a pear.

But the good honest old women who sat about

in the Grande Place, hearing, had always taken the fruit-girl to task, when they got her by herself.

"Leave the child alone, you mischievous one," said they. "Be content with being base yourself. Look you, Lisette—she is not one like you to make eyes at the law-students, and pester the painter lads for a day's outing. Let her be, or we will tell your mother how you leave the fruit for the gutter children to pick and thieve, while you are stealing up the stairs into that young French fellow's chamber. Oh, oh! a fine beating you will get when she knows!"

Lisette's mother was a fierce and strong old Brabantoise, who exacted heavy reckoning with her daughter for every single plum and peach that she sent out of her dark sweet-smelling fruit-shop to be sunned in the streets, and under the students' love-glances.

So the girl took heed, and left Bébée alone.

"What should I want her to come with us for?" she reasoned with herself. "She is twice as pretty as I am; Jules might take to her instead—who knows?"

So that she was at once savage and yet triumphant when she saw, as she thought, Bébée drifting down the high flood of temptation.

"Oh, oh, you dainty one!" she cried one day to her. "So you would not take the nuts and mulberries that do for us common folk, because you had a mind for a fine pine out of the hothouses!

That was all, was it? Eh, well—I do not begrudge you. Only take care; remember, the nuts and mulberries last through summer and autumn, and there are heaps of them on every fair-stall and street-corner; but the pine—that is eaten in a day, one spring-time, and its like does not grow in the hedges. You will have your mouth full of sugar an hour—and then, eh!—you will go famished all the year."

"I do not understand," said Bébée, looking up, with her thoughts far away, and scarcely hearing the words spoken to her.

"Oh, pretty little fool! you understand well enough," said Lisette, grinning, as she rubbed up a melon. "Does he give you fine things? You might let me see."

"No one gives me anything."

"Chut! you want me to believe that. Why Jules is only a lad, and his father is a silk-mercer, and only gives him a hundred francs a month, but Jules buys me all I want—somehow—or do you think I would take the trouble to set my cap straight when he goes by? He gave me these ear-rings, look. I wish you would let me see what you get."

But Bébée had gone away—unheeding—dreaming of Juliet and of Jeanne d'Arc, of whom he had told her tales.

He made sketches of her sometimes, but seldom pleased himself.

It was not so easy as he had imagined that it would prove to portray this little flower-like face, with the clear eyes and the child's open brow. He who had painted Phryne so long and faithfully had got a taint on his brush—he could not paint this pure, bright, rosy dawn — he who had always painted the glare of midnight gas on rouge or rags. Yet he felt that if he could transfer to canvas the light that was on Bébée's face he would get what Scheffer had missed. For a time it eluded him. You shall paint a gold and glistening brocade, or a fan of peacock's feathers, to perfection, and yet, perhaps, the dewy whiteness of the humble little field-daisy shall baffle and escape you.

He felt, too, that he must catch her expression flying as he would do the flash of a swallow's wing across a blue sky; he knew that Bébée, forced to studied attitudes in an atelier, would be no longer the ideal that he wanted.

More than once he came and filled in more fully his various designs in the little hut garden, among the sweet gray lavender and the golden disks of the sunflowers; and more than once Bebée was missed from her place in the front of the Broodhuis.

The Varnhart children would gather now and then open-mouthed at the wicket, and Mère Krebs would shake her head as she went by on her sheepskin saddle, and mutter that the child's head would be turned by vanity; and old Jehan would lean on his stick and peer through the sweet-brier, and wonder stupidly if this strange man who could make Bébée's face beam over again upon that panel of wood could not give him back his dead daughter who had been pushed away under the black earth so long, long before, when the red mill had been brave and new, the red mill that the boys and girls called old.

But except these, no one noticed much.

Painters were no rare sights in Brabant.

The people were used to see them coming and going, making pictures of mud and stones, and ducks and sheep, and of all common and silly things.

"What does he pay you, Bébée?" they used to ask, with the shrewd Flemish thought after the main chance.

"Nothing," Bébée would answer, with a quick color in her face; and they would reply in contemptuous reproof, "Careless little fool; — you should make enough to buy you wood all winter. When the man from Ghent painted Trine and her cow, he gave her a whole gold bit for standing still so long in the clover. The Krebs would be sure to lend you her cow if it be the cow that makes the difference."

Bébée was silent, weeding her carnation-bed;— what could she tell them that they would understand?

She seemed so far away from them all—those good friends of her childhood—now that this wonderful new world of his giving had opened to her sight.

She lived in a dream.

Whether she sat in the market-place taking copper coins, or in the moonlight with a book on her knees, it was all the same. Her feet ran, her tongue spoke, her hands worked; she did not neglect her goat or her garden, she did not forsake her house labor or her good deeds to old Annémie; but all the while she only heard one voice, she only felt one touch, she only saw one face.

Here and there—one in a million—there is a female thing that can love like this, once and for ever.

Such an one is dedicated, birth upwards, to the Mater Dolorosa.

He had something nearer akin to affection for her than he had ever had in his life for anything, but he was never in love with her—no more in love with her than with the moss-rosebuds that she fastened in his breast. Yet he played with her, because she was such a little, soft, tempting, female thing; and because, to see her face flush, and her heart heave, to feel her fresh feelings stir into life, and to watch her changes from shyness to confidence, and from frankness again into fear, was a natural pastime in the lazy golden weather.

That he spared her as far as he did—when after all she would have married Jeannot anyhow,—and that he sketched her face in the open air, and never entered her hut and never beguiled her to his own old palace in the city, was a new virtue in himself for which he hardly knew whether to feel respect or ridicule; anyway it seemed virtue to him.

So long as he did not seduce the body it seemed to him that it could never matter how he slew the soul—the little, honest, happy, pure, frank soul, that amidst its poverty and hardships was like a robin's song to the winter sun.

"Hoot, toot, pretty innocent, so you are no better than the rest of us," hissed her enemy, Lisette, the fruit-girl, against her as she went by the stall one evening as the sun set. "Prut! so it was no such purity after all that made you never look at the student lads and the soldiers, eh?—You were so dainty of taste, you must needs pick and choose, and, Lord's sake, after all your coyness, to drop at a beckoning finger as one may say—pong!—in a minute, like an apple over-ripe! Oh hé, you sly one!"

Bébée flushed red, in a sort of instinct of offense; not sure what her fault was, but vaguely stung by the brutal words.

Bébée walked homeward by him, with her empty baskets: looked at him with grave wondering eyes.

"What did she mean? I do not understand. I must have done some wrong—or she thinks so. Do you know?——"

Flamen laughed, and answered her evasively:

"You have done her the wrong of a fair skin when hers is brown, and a little foot while hers is as big as a trooper's; there is no greater sin, Bébée, possible in woman to woman."

"Hold your peace, you shrill jade," he added, in

anger to the fruiterer, flinging at her a crown piece, that the girl caught, and bit with her teeth with a chuckle. "Do not heed her, Bébée. She is a coarse-tongued brute, and is jealous, no doubt."

"Jealous?—of what?"

The word had no meaning to Bébée.

"That I am not a student or a soldier, as her lovers are."

As her lovers were! Bébée felt her face burn again. Was he her lover then? The child's innocent body and soul thrilled with a hot, sweet delight and fear commingled.

Bébée was not quite satisfied until she had knelt down that night and asked the Master of all poor maidens to see if there were any wickedness in her heart, hidden there like a bee in a rose, and if there were to take it out and make her worthier of this wonderful new happiness in her life.

CHAPTER XIV.

THE next day, waking with a radiant little soul as a bird in a forest wakes in summer, Bébée was all alone in the lane by the swans' water. In the gray of the dawn all the good folk except herself and lame old Jehan had tramped off to a pilgrimage, Liège way, which the bishop of the city had enjoined on all the faithful as a sacred duty.

Bébée doing her work, singing, thinking how good God was, and dreaming over a thousand fancies of the wonderful stories he had told her, and of the exquisite delight that would lie for her in watching for him all through the shining hours, Bébée felt her little heart leap like a squirrel as the voice that was the music of heaven to her called through the stillness,—

"Good-day, pretty one! you are as early as the lark, Bébée. I go to Mayence, so I thought I would look at you one moment as I pass."

Bébée ran down through the wet grass in a tumult of joy. She had never seen him so early in the day—never so early as this, when nobody was up and stirring except birds and beasts and peasant folk.

She did not know how pretty she looked herself; like a rain-washed wild rose; her feet gleaming with dew, her cheeks warm with health and joy; her sunny clustering hair free from the white cap and tumbling a little about her throat, because she had been stooping over the carnations.

Flamen loosed the wicket latch, and thought there might be better ways of spending the day than in the gray shadows of old Mechlin.

"Will you give me a draught of water?" he asked her as he crossed the garden.

"I will give you breakfast," said Bébée, happy as a bird. She felt no shame for the smallness of her home; no confusion at the poverty of her little place; such embarrassments are born of self-consciousness, and Bébée had no more self-consciousness than her own sweet, gray lavender-bush blowing against the door.

The lavender-bush has no splendor like the roses, has no colors like the hollyhocks; it is a simple, plain, gray thing that the bees love and that the cottagers cherish, and that keeps the moth from the homespun linen, and that goes with the dead to their graves.

It has many virtues and infinite sweetness, but it does not know it or think of it; and if the village girls ever tell it so, it fancies they only praise it out of kindness as they put its slender fragrant spears away in their warm bosoms. Bébée was like her lavender, and now that this beautiful Purple Emperor butterfly came from the golden sunbeams to find pleasure for a second in her freshness, she was only very grateful, as the lavender-bush was to the village girls.

"I will give you your breakfast," said Bébée, flushing rosily with pleasure, and putting away the ivy coils that he might enter.

"I have very little, you know," she added, wistfully. "Only goat's milk and bread; but if that will do—and there is some honey—and if you would eat a salad, I would cut one fresh."

He did enter, and glanced round him with a curious pity and wonder both in one.

It was such a little, small, square place; and its floor was of beaten clay; and its unceiled roof he could have touched; and its absolute poverty was so plain,—and yet the child looked so happy in it, and was so like a flower, and was so dainty and fresh, and even so full of grace.

She stood and looked at him with frank and grateful eyes; she could hardly believe that he was here; he, the stranger of Rubes' land, in her own little rush-covered home.

But she was not embarrassed by it; she was glad and proud.

There is a dignity of peasants as well as of kings —the dignity that comes from all absence of effort, all freedom from pretense. Bébée had this, and she had more still than this: she had the absolute simplicity of childhood with her still.

Some women have it still when they are fourscore.

She could have looked at him forever, she was so happy; she cared nothing now for those dazzling dahlias—he had left them; he was actually here—here in her own, little, dear home, with the cocks looking in at the threshold, and the sweet-peas nodding at the lattice, and the starling crying "Bonjour! Bonjour!"

"You are tired, I am sure you must be tired," she said, pulling her little bed forward for him to sit on, for there were only two wooden stools in the hut, and no chair at all.

Then she took his sketching-easel and brushes from his hand, and would have kneeled and taken the dust off his boots if he would have let her; and went hither and thither gladly and lightly, bringing him a wooden bowl of milk and the rest of the slender fare, and cutting as quick as thought fresh cresses and lettuce from her garden, and bringing him, as the crown of all, Father Francis's honey-comb on vine-leaves, with some pretty sprays of box and mignonette scattered about it — doing all this with a swift, sweet grace that robbed the labor of all look of servitude, and looking at him ever and again with a smile that said as clearly as any words, "I cannot do much, but what I do, I do with all my heart."

There was something in the sight of her going and coming in those simple household errands, across the sunlit floor, that moved him as some mountain air sung on an alp by a girl driving her cows to pasture may move a listener who indifferent has heard the swell of the organ of La Hague, or the recitative of a great singer in San Carlo.

The gray lavender blowing at the house-door has its charm for those who are tired of the camellias that float in the porcelain bowls of midnight suppers.

This man was not good. He was idle and vain, and amorous and cold, and had been spoiled by the world in which he had passed his days; but he had the temper of an artist; he had something, too, of a poet's fancy; he was vaguely touched and won by this simple soul that looked at him out of Bébée's eyes with some look that in all its simplicity had a divine gleam in it that made him half ashamed.

He had known women by the thousand, good women and bad; women whom he had dealt ill with and women who had dealt ill with him; but this he had not known — this frank, fearless, tender, gay, grave, innocent, industrious little life, helping itself, feeding itself, defending itself, working for itself and for others, and vaguely seeking all the while some unseen light, some unknown god, with a blind faith so infinitely ignorant and yet so infinitely pathetic.

"All the people are gone on a pilgrimage," she explained to him when he asked her why her village was so silent this bright morning. "They are gone to pray for a fine harvest, and then each one prays for some other little thing that she wants herself as well—it costs seven francs apiece.

They take their food with them; they go and laugh and eat in the fields. I think it is nonsense. One can say one's prayers just as well here. Mère Krebs thinks so too, but then she says, 'If I do not go, it will look ill; people will say I am irreligious; and as we make so much by flour, God would think it odd for me to be absent; and, besides, it is only seven francs there and back; and if it does please Heaven, that is cheap, you know. One will get it over and over again in Paradise.' That is what Mère Krebs says. But, for me, I think it is nonsense. It cannot please God to go by train and eat galette and waste a whole day in getting dusty.

"When I give the Virgin my cactus flower, I do give up a thing I love, and I let it wither on her altar instead of pleasing me in bloom here all the week, and then, of course, she sees that I have done it out of gratitude. But that is different: that I am sorry to do, and yet I am glad to do it out of love. Do you not know?"

"Yes, I know very well. But is the Virgin all that you love like this?"

"No; there is the garden, and there is Antoine—he is dead, I know. But I think that we should love the dead all the better, not the less, because they cannot speak or say that they are angry; and perhaps one pains them very much when one neglects them, and if they are ever so sad, they cannot rise and rebuke one—that is why I would rather forget the flowers for the Church than I would the flowers for his grave, because God can punish me, of course, if he like, but Antoine never can—any more—now."

"You are logical in your sentiment, my dear," said Flamen, who was more moved than he cared to feel. "The union is a rare one in your sex. Who taught you to reason?"

"No one. And I do not know what to be logical means. Is it that you laugh at me?"

"No. I do not laugh. And your pilgrims—they are gone for all day?"

"Yes. They are gone to the Sacred Heart at St. Marie en Bois. It is on the way to Liége. They will come back at night-fall. And some of them will be sure to have drunk too much, and the children will get so cross. Prosper Bar, who is a Calvinist, always says, 'Do not mix up prayer and play; you would not cut a gherkin in your honey;' but I do not know why he called prayer a gherkin, because it is sweet enough—sweeter than anything, I think. When I pray to the Virgin to let me see you next day, I go to bed quite happy, because she will do it, I know, if it will be good for me."

"But if it were not good for you, Bébée? Would you cease to wish it then?"

He rose as he spoke, and went across the floor and drew away her hand that was parting the flax, and took it in his own and stroked it, indulgently and carelessly, as a man may stroke the soft fur of a young cat.

Leaning against the little lattice and looking down on her with musing eyes, half smiling, half serious, half amorous, half sad, Bébée looked up with a sudden and delicious terror that ran through her as the charm of the snake's gaze runs through the bewildered bird.

"Would you cease to wish if it were not good?" he asked again.

Bébée's face grew pale and troubled. She left her hand in his because she did not think any shame of his taking it. But the question suddenly flung the perplexity and darkness of doubt into the clearness of her pure child's conscience. All her ways had been straight and sunlit before her.

She had never had a divided duty.

The religion and the pleasure of her simple little life had always gone hand-in-hand, greeting one another, and never for an instant in conflict. In any hesitation of her own she had always gone to Father Francis, and he had disentangled the web for her and made all plain.

But here was a difficulty in which she could never go to Father Francis.

Right and wrong, duty and desire, were for the first time arrayed before her in their ghastly and unending warfare.

It frightened her with a certain breathless sense of peril—the peril of a time when in lieu of that gentle Mother of Roses whom she kneeled to among the flowers, she would only see a dusky shadow looming between her and the beauty of life and the light of the sun.

What he said was quite vague to her. She attached no definite danger to his words. She only thought—to see him was so great a joy—if Mary forbade it, would she not take it if she could notwithstanding, always, always, always?

He kept her hand in his, and watched with contentment the changing play of the shade and sorrow, the fear and fascination, on her face.

"You do not know, Bébée?" he said at length, knowing well himself; so much better than ever she knew. "Well, dear—that is not flattering to me. But it is natural. The good Virgin of course gives you all you have, food, and clothes, and your garden, and your pretty plump chickens—and I am only a stranger. You could not offend her for me—that is not likely."

The child was cut to the heart by the sadness and humility of words of whose studied artifice she had no suspicion.

She thought that she seemed to him ungrateful and selfish, and yet all the mooring-ropes that held her little boat of life to the harbor of its simple religion seemed cut away, and she seemed drifting helpless and rudderless upon an unknown sea.

"I never did do wrong—that I know," she said timidly, and lifted her eyes to his with an unconscious appeal in them.

"But—I do not see why it should be wrong to speak with you. You are good, and you lend me beautiful things out of other men's minds that will make me less ignorant: Our Lady could not be angry with that—she must like it."

"Our Lady?—oh, poor little simpleton!—where will her reign be when Ignorance has once been cut down, root and branch?" he thought to himself; but he only answered,—

"But whether she like it or not, Bébée?—you beg the question, my dear; you are—you are not so frank as usual—think, and tell me honestly?"

He knew quite well, but it amused him to see the perplexed trouble that this, the first divided duty of her short years, brought with it.

Bébée looked at him, and loosened her hand from his, and sat quite still. Her lips had a little quiver in them.

"I think," she said at last, "I think—if it *be* wrong, still I will wish it—yes. Only I will not tell myself it is right. I will just say to Our Lady, 'I am wicked, perhaps, but I cannot help it.' So—I will not deceive her at all; and perhaps in time she may forgive. But I think you only say it to try me. It cannot, I am sure, be wrong—any more than it is to talk to Jeannot or to Bac."

He had driven her into the subtleties of doubt, but the honest little soul in her found a way out, as a flower in a cellar finds its way through the stones to light.

He plucked the ivy-leaves and threw them at the chickens on the bricks without, with a certain impatience in the action. The simplicity and the directness of the answer disarmed him; he was almost ashamed to use against her the weapons of his habitual warfare. It was like a maître d'armes fencing with bare steel against a little naked child armed with a blest palm-sheaf.

When she had thus brought him all she had, and he to please her had sat down to the simple food, she gathered a spray of roses and set it in a pot beside him, then left him and went and stood at a little distance, waiting, with her hands lightly crossed on her chest, to see if there were anything that he might want.

He ate and drank well to please her, looking at her often as he did so.

"I break your bread, Bébée," he said, with a tone that seemed strange to her. "I break your bread. I must keep Arab faith with you."

"What is that?"

"I mean—I must never betray you."

"Betray me! How could you?"

"Well—hurt you in any way."

"Ah, I am sure you would never do that."

He was silent, and looked at the spray of roses.

"Sit down and spin," he said impatiently. "I am ashamed to see you stand there, and a woman never looks so well as when she spins. Sit down —and I will eat the good things you have brought me. But I cannot if you stand and look."

"I beg your pardon, I did not know," she said, ashamed lest she should have seemed rude to him; and she drew out her wheel under the light of the lattice, and sat down to it, and began to disentangle the threads.

It was a pretty picture—the low, square casement; the frame of ivy, the pink and white of the climbing sweet-peas; the girl's head; the cool, wet leaves; the old wooden spinning-wheel, that purred like a sleepy cat.

"I want to paint you as Gretchen, only it will be a shame," he said.

"Who is Gretchen?"

"You shall read of her by-and-by. And you live here all by yourself?"

"Since Antoine died—yes."

"And are never dull?"

"I have no time, and I do not think I would be if I had time—there is so much to think of, and one never can understand."

"But you must be very brave and laborious to do all your work yourself. Is it possible a child like you can spin, and wash, and bake, and garden, and do everything?"

"Oh, many do more than I. Babette's eldest daughter is only twelve, and she does much more, because she has all the children to look after; and they are very, very poor; they often have nothing but a stew of nettles and perhaps a few snails, days together."

"That is lean, bare, ugly, gruesome poverty; there is plenty of that everywhere. But you, Bébée—you are an idyll."

Bébée looked across the hut and smiled, and

broke her thread. She did not know what he meant, but if she were anything that pleased him, it was well.

"Who were those beautiful women?" she said suddenly, the color mounting into her cheeks.

"What women, my dear?"

"Those I saw at the window with you, the other night—they had jewels."

"Oh!—women, tiresome enough; if I had seen you, I would have dropped you some fruit. Poor little Bébée! Did you go by, and I never knew?"

"You were laughing——"

"Was I?"

"Yes, and they *were* beautiful."

"In their own eyes; not in mine."

"No?"

She stopped her spinning and gazed at him with wistful, wondering eyes. Could it be that they were not beautiful to him? those deep red, glowing, sun-basked dahlia flowers?

"Do you know," she said very softly, with a flush of penitence that came and went, "when I saw them, I hated them; I confessed it to Father Francis next day. You seemed so content with them, and they looked so gay and glad there—and then the jewels! Somehow, I seemed to myself such a little thing, and so ugly and mean. And yet, do you know——"

"And yet—well?"

"They did not look to me good—those women," said Bébée thoughtfully, looking across at him in deprecation of his possible anger. "They wer great people, I suppose, and they appeared very happy; but though I seemed nothing to myself after them, still I think I would not change."

"You are wise without books, Bébée."

"Oh, no—I am not wise at all. I only feel. And give me books; oh, pray, give me books! You do not know; I will learn so fast—and I will not neglect anything, that I promise. The neighbors and Jeannot say that I shall let the flowers die, and the hut get dirty, and never spin or prick Annémie's patterns; but that is untrue. I will do all, just as I have done, and more too, if only you will give me things to read, for I do think when one is happy, one ought to work more—not less."

"But will these books make you happy? If you ask me the truth, I must tell you—no. You are happy as you are, because you know nothing else than your own little life; for ignorance *is* happiness, Bébée, let sages, ancient and modern, say what they will. But when you know a little, you will want to know more; and when you know much you will want to see much also, and then—and then—the thing will grow—you will be no longer content. That is, you will be unhappy."

Bébée watched him with wistful eyes.

"Perhaps that it is true. No doubt it is true, if you say it. But you know all the world seems full of voices that I hear, but that I cannot understand; it is with me as I should think it is with people who go to foreign countries and do not know the tongue that is spoken when they land; and it makes me unhappy, because I cannot comprehend, and so the books will not make me more so, but less. And as for being content—when I thought you were gone away out of the city, last night, I thought I would never be able to pray any more, because I hated myself, and I almost hated the angels, and I told Mary that she was cruel, and she turned her face from me—as it seemed, forever."

She spoke quite quietly and simply, spinning as she spoke, and looking across at him with earnest eyes, that begged him to believe her. She was saying the pure truth, but she did not know the force or the meaning of that truth.

He listened with a smile; it was not new to him; he knew her heart much better than she knew it herself, but there was an unconsciousness, and yet a strength, in the words that touched him though.

He threw the leaves away, irritably, and told her to leave off her spinning.

"Some day I shall paint you with that wheel as I painted the Broodhuis. Will you let me, Bébée?"

"Yes."

She answered him as she would have answered if he had told her to go on pilgrimage from one end of the Low Countries to the other.

"What were you going to do to-day?"

"I am going into the market with the flowers; I go every day."

"How much will you make?"

"Two or three francs, if I am lucky."

"And do you never have a holiday?"

"Oh, yes; but not often, you know, because it is on the fête days that the people want the most flowers."

"But in the winter?"

"Then I work at the lace."

"Do you never go into the woods?"

"I have been, once or twice; but it loses a whole day."

"You are afraid of not earning?"

"Yes. Because I am afraid of owing people anything."

"Well, give up this one day, and we will make holiday. The people are out; they will not know. Come into the forest, and we will dine at a café in the woods; and we will be as poetic as you like, and I will tell you a tale of one called Rosalind, who pranked herself in boy's attire, all for love, in the Ardennes country yonder. Come, it is the very day for the forest; it will make me a lad again at Meudon, when the lilacs were in bloom. Poor Paris! Come."

"Do you mean it?"

The color was bright in her face, her heart was dancing, her little feet felt themselves already on the fresh green turf.

She had no thought that there could be any harm in it. She would have gone with Jeannot or old Bac.

"Of course I mean it. Come. I was going to Mayence to see the Magi and Van Dyck's Christ. We will go to Soignies instead, and study green leaves. I will paint your face by sunlight. It is the best way to paint you. You belong to the open air. So should Gretchen; or how else should she have the blue sky in her eyes?"

"But I have only wooden shoes!"

Her face was scarlet as she glanced at her feet; he who had wanted to give her the silk stockings—how would he like to be seen walking abroad with those two clumsy, clattering, work-a-day, little sabots?

"Never mind. My dear, in my time I have had enough of satin shoes and of silver gilt heels; they click-clack as loud as yours, and cost much more to those who walk with them, not to mention that they will seldom deign to walk at all. Your wooden shoes are picturesque. Paganini made a violin out of a wooden shoe. Who knows what music may lurk in yours, only you have never heard it. Perhaps I have. It was Bac who gave you the red shoes that was the barbarian, not I. Come."

"You really mean it?"

"Come."

"But they will miss me at market."

"They will think you are gone on the pilgrimage: you need never tell them you have not."

"But if they ask me?"

"Does it never happen that you say any other thing than the truth?"

"Any other thing than the truth! Of course not. People take for granted that one tells truth; it would be very base to cheat them. Do you really mean that I may come?—in the forest!—and you will tell me stories like those you give me to read?"

"I will tell you a better story. Lock your hut, Bébée, and come."

"And to think you are not ashamed!"

"Ashamed?"

"Yes, because of my wooden shoes."

Was it possible? Bébée thought, as she ran out into the garden and locked the door behind her, and pushed the key under the water-butt as usual, being quite content with that prudent precaution against robbers which had served Antoine all his days. Was it possible, this wonderful joy?—her cheeks were like her roses, her eyes had a brilliance like the sun; the natural grace and mirth of the child blossomed in a thousand ways and gestures.

As she went by the shrine in the wall, she bent her knee a moment and made the sign of the cross; then she gathered a little moss-rose that nodded close under the border of the palisade, and turned and gave it to him.

"Look, she sends you this. She is not angry, you see, and it is much more pleasure when she is pleased—do you not know?"

He shrank a little as her fingers touched him.

"What a pity you had no mother, Bébée!" he said, on an impulse of emotion, of which in Paris he would have been more ashamed than of any guilt.

CHAPTER XV.

IN the deserted lane by the swans' water, under the willows, the horses waited to take him to Mechlin; little, quick, rough horses, with round brass bells, in the Flemish fashion, and gay harness, and a low char-à-banc, in which a wolf-skin and red rugs, and all a painter's many necessities, were tossed together.

He lifted her in, and the little horses flew fast through the green country, ringing chimes at each step, till they plunged into the deep glades of the woods of Cambre and Soignies.

Bébée sat breathless with delight.

She had never gone behind horses in all her life, except once or twice in a wagon when the tired teamsters had dragged a load of corn across the plains, or when the miller's old gray mare had hobbled wearily before a cart-load of noisy, happy, mischievous children going home from the masses and fairs, and flags, and flowers, and church banners, and puppet-shows, and lighted altars, and whirling merry-go-rounds of the Fête Dieu.

She had never known what it was to sail as on the wings of the wind along broad roads, with yellow wheat-lands, and green hedges, and wayside trees, and little villages, and reedy canal-water, all flying by her to the sing-song of the joyous bells.

"Oh, how good it is to live!" she cried, clapping her hands in a very ecstasy, as the clear morning broadened into gold and the west wind rose and blew from the sands by the sea.

"Yes—it is good—if one did not tire so soon," said he, watching her with a listless pleasure.

But she did not hear; she was beyond the reach of any power to sadden her; she was watching the white oxen that stood on the purple brow of the just reapen lands, and the rosy clouds that blew like a shower of apple-blossoms across the sky to the south.

There was a sad darkling Calvary on the edge of the harvest-field that looked black against the blue sky; its shadow fell across the road, but she did not see it: she was looking at the sun.

There is not much change in the great Soignies woods. They are aisles on aisles of beautiful green trees, crossing and recrossing; tunnels of dark foliage that look endless; long avenues of beech, of oak, of elm, or of fir, with the bracken and the brushwood growing dense between; a delicious forest-growth everywhere, shady even at noon, and by a little past midday dusky as evening; with the forest fragrance, sweet and dewy, all about, and under the fern the stirring of wild game, and the white gleam of little rabbits, and the sound of the wings of birds.

Soignies is not legend-haunted like the Black Forest, nor king-haunted like Fontainebleau, nor sovereign of two historic streams like the brave woods of Heidelberg; nor wild and romantic, and broken with black rocks, and poetized by the shade of Jaques, and swept through by a perfect river, like its neighbors of Ardennes; nor throned aloft on mighty mountains like the majestic oak-glades of the Swabian hills of the ivory-carvers.

Soignies is only a Flemish forest in a plain, throwing its shadow over corn-fields and cattle pastures, with no panorama beyond it and no wonders in its depth. But it is a fresh, bold, beautiful forest for all that.

It has only green leaves to give — green leaves always, league after league; but there is about it that vague mystery which all forests have, and this universe of leaves seems boundless, and Pan might dwell in it, and St. Hubert, and John Keats.

Bébée, in her rare holidays with the Bac children or with Jeannot's sisters, had never penetrated farther than the glades of the Cambre, and had never entered the heart of the true forest, which is much still what it must have been in the old days when the burghers of Brabant cut their yew bows and their pike-staves from it to use against the hosts of Spain.

To Bébée it was as an enchanted land, and every play of light and shade, every hare speeding across the paths, every thrush singing in the leaves, every little dog-rose or harebell that blossomed in the thickets, was to her a treasure, a picture, a poem, a delight.

He had seen girls thus in the woods of Vincennes and of Versailles in the student days of his youth; little work-girls fresh from châlets of the Jura or from vine-hung huts of the Loire, who had brought their poor little charms to perish in Paris; and who dwelt under the hot tiles and amidst the gilded shop signs till they were as pale and thin as their own starved balsams; and who, when they saw the green woods, laughed and cried a little, and thought of the broad sun-swept fields, and wished that they were back again behind their drove of cows, or weeding among the green grapes.

But those little work-girls had been mere homely daisies, and daisies already with the dust of the pavement and of the dancing-gardens upon them.

Bébée was as pure and fresh as these dew-wet dog-roses that she found in the thickets of thorn.

He had meant to treat her as he had used to do those work-girls—a little wine, a little wooing, a little folly and passion, idle as a butterfly and brief as a rainbow—one midsummer day and night—then a handful of gold, a caress, a good-morrow, and forgetfulness ever afterwards—that was what he had meant when he had brought her out to the forest of Soignies.

But—she was different, this child.

He made the great sketch of her for his Gretchen, sitting on a moss-ground trunk, with marguerites in her hand; he sent for their breakfast far into the woods, and saw her set her pearly teeth into early peaches and costly sweatmeats; he wandered with her hither and thither, and told her tales out of the poets and talked to her in the dreamy, cynical, poetical manner that was characteristic of him, being half artificial and half sorrowful, as his temper was.

But Bébée — all unconscious, intoxicated with happiness, and yet touched by it into that vague sadness which the summer sun brings with it even to young things, if they have soul in them;— Bébée said to him what the work-girls of Paris never had done.

Beautiful things: things fantastic, ignorant, absurd, very simple, very unreasonable oftentimes, but things beautiful always, and sometimes even very wise by a wisdom not of the world; by a certain light divine that does shine now and then as through an alabaster lamp, through minds that have no grossness to obscure them.

Her words were not equal to the burden of her thoughts at times, but he knew how to take the pearl of the thought from the broken shell and tangled sea-weed of her simple, untutored speech.

"If there be a God anywhere," he thought to himself, "this little Fleming is very near him."

She was so near that although he had no belief in any God, he could not deal with her as he had used to do with the work-girls in the primrose paths of old Vincennes.

CHAPTER XVI.

"TO be Gretchen, you must count the leaves of your daisies," he said to her, as he painted — painted her just as she was, with her two little white feet in the wooden shoes, and the thick, green leaves behind; the simplest picture possible, the dress of gray—only cool dark gray—with white linen bodice, and no color anywhere except in the green of the foliage; but where he meant the wonder and the charm of it to lie was in the upraised, serious, child-like face, and the gaze of the grave, smiling eyes.

It was Gretchen, spinning, out in the open air among the flowers. Gretchen, with the tall dog-daisies growing up about her feet, among the thyme and the roses, before she had had need to gather one to ask her future of its parted leaves.

The Gretchen of Scheffer tells no tale; she is a fair-haired, hard-working, simple-minded peasant, with whom neither angels nor devils have anything to do, and whose eyes never can open to either hell or heaven. But the Gretchen of Flamen said much more than this: looking at it, men would sigh from shame, and women weep from sorrow.

"Count the daisies?" echoed Bébée. "Oh, I know what you mean. A little—much—passionately—until death—not at all. What the girls say when they want to see if any one loves them? Is that it?"

She looked at him without any consciousness—except as she loved the flowers.

"Do you think the daisies know?" she went on, seriously, parting their petals with her fingers. "Flowers do know many things—that is certain."

"Ask them for yourself."

"Ask them what?"

"How much—any one—loves you?"

"Oh, but every one loves me; there is no one that is bad. Antoine used to say to me, 'Never think of yourself, Bébée; always think of other people, so every one will love you.' And I always try to do that, and every one does."

"But that is not the love the daisy tells of to your sex."

"No?"

"No; the girls that you see count the flowers—they are thinking, not of all the village, but of some one unlike all the rest, whose shadow falls across theirs in the moonlight! You know that?"

"Ah, yes—and they marry afterwards—yes."

She said it softly, musingly, with no embarrassment; it was an unreal, remote thing to her, and yet it stirred her heart a little with a vague trouble that was infinitely sweet.

There is little talk of love in the lives of the

poor; they have no space for it; love to them means more mouths to feed, more wooden shoes to buy, more hands to dive into the meagre bag of coppers. Now and then a girl of the commune had been married, and had gone out just the same the next day to her plowing in the fields or to her lace-weaving in the city. Bébée had thought little of it.

"They marry or they do not marry. That is as it may be," said Flamen, with a smile. "Bébée, I must paint you as Gretchen before she made a love-dial of the daisies. What is the story? Oh, I have told you stories enough. Gretchen's you would not understand, just yet."

"But what did the daisies say to her?"

"My dear, the daisies always say the same thing, because daisies always tell the truth and know men. The daisies always say 'a little;' it is the girl's ear that tricks her, and makes her hear 'till death,'—a folly and falsehood of which the daisy is not guilty."

"But who says it if the daisy do not?"

"Ah, the devil perhaps—who knows? He has so much to do in these things."

But Bébée did not smile; she had a look of horror in her blue eyes; she belonged to a peasantry who believed in exorcising the fiend by the aid of the cross, and who not so very many generations before had driven him out of human bodies by rack and flame.

She looked with a little wistful fear on the

white, golden-eyed marguerites that lay on her lap.

"Do you think the fiend is in these?" she whispered, with awe in her voice.

Flamen smiled. "When you count them he will be there, no doubt."

Bébée threw them with a shudder on the grass.

"Have I spoilt your holiday, dear?" he said, with a certain self-reproach.

She was silent a minute, then she gathered up the daisies again, and stroked them and put them to her lips.

"It is not they that do wrong. You say the girls' ears deceive them. It is the girls who want a lie and will not believe a truth because it humbles them; it is the girls that are to blame, not the daisies. As for me, I will not ask the daisies anything ever, so the fiend will not enter into them."

"Nor into you. Poor little Bébée!"

"Why, you pity me for that?"

"Yes. Because, if women never see the serpent's face, neither do they ever scent the smell of the paradise roses; and it will be hard for you to die without a single rose d'amour in your pretty breast, poor little Bébée?"

"I do not understand. But you frighten me a little."

He rose and left his easel and threw himself at her feet on the grass; he took the little wooden shoes in his hands as reverently as he would have taken the broidered shoes of a duchess; he looked up at her with tender, smiling eyes.

"Poor little Bébée!" he said again. "Did I frighten you indeed? Nay, that was very base of me. We will not spoil our summer holiday. There is no such thing as a fiend, my dear. There are only men—such as I am. Say the daisy spell over for me, Bébée. See if I do not love you a little, just as you love your flowers."

She smiled, and the happy laughter came again over her face.

"Oh, I am sure you care for me a little," she said, softly, "or you would not be so good and get me books and give me pleasure; and I do not want the daisies to tell me that, because you say it yourself, which is better."

"Much better," he answered her dreamily, and lay there in the grass, holding the little wooden shoes in his hands.

He was not in love with her. He was in no haste. He preferred to play with her softly, slowly, as one separates the leaves of a rose, to see the deep rose of its heart.

Her own ignorance of what she felt had a charm for him. He liked to lift the veil from her eyes by gentle degrees, watching each new pulse-beat, each fresh instinct tremble into life.

It was an old, old story to him; he knew each chapter and verse to weariness, though there still was no other story that he still read as often. But to her it was so new.

To him it was a long beaten track; he knew every turn of it; he recognized every wayside blossom; he had passed over a thousand times each tremulous bridge; he knew so well beforehand where each shadow would fall, and where each fresh bud would blossom, and where each harvest would be reaped.

But to her it was so new.

She followed him as a blind child a man that guides her through a garden and reads her a wonder tale.

He was good to her, that was all she knew. When he touched her ever so lightly she felt a happiness so perfect, and yet so unintelligible, that she could have wished to die in it.

And in her humility and her ignorance she wondered always how he—so great, so wise, so beautiful—could have thought it ever worth his while to leave the paradise of Rubes' land to wait with her under her little rush-thatched roof, and bring her here to see the green leaves and the living things of the forest.

As they went, a man was going under the trees with a load of wood upon his back. Bébée gave a little cry of recognition.

"Oh, look, that is Jeannot! How he will wonder to see me here!"

Flamen drew her a little downward, so that the forester passed onward without perceiving them.

"Why do you do that?" said Bébée. "Shall I not speak to him?"

"Why? To have all your neighbors chatter of your feast in the forest? It is not worth while."

"Ah, but I always tell them everything," said Bébée, whose imagination had been already busy with the wonders that she would unfold to Mère Krebs and the Varnhart children.

"Then you will see but little of me, my dear. Learn to be silent, Bébée. It is a woman's first duty, though her hardest."

"Is it?"

She did not speak for some time. She could not imagine a state of things in which she would not narrate the little daily miracles of her life to the good old garrulous women and the little open-mouthed romps. And yet—she lifted her eyes to his.

"I am glad you have told me that," she said. "Though indeed, I do not see why one should not say what one does, yet—somehow—I do not like to talk about you. It is like the pictures in the galleries, and the music in the cathedral, and the great still evenings, when the fields are all silent, and it is as if Christ walked abroad in them;—I do not know how to talk of those things to the others—only to you—and I do not like to talk *about* you to them—do you not know?"

"Yes, I know. But what affinity have I, Bébée, to your thoughts of your God walking in His corn-fields?"

Bébée's eyes glanced down through the green aisle of the forests, with the musing seriousness in them that was like the child-angels of Botticelli's dreams.

"I cannot tell you very well. But when I am in the fields at evening and think of Christ, I feel so happy, and of such good will to all the rest, and I seem to see heaven quite plain through the beautiful gray air where the stars are—and so I feel when I am with you—that is all. Only——"

"Only what?"

"Only in those evenings, when I was all alone, heaven seemed up there, where the stars are, and I longed for wings; but now, it is *here*—and I would only shut my wings if I had them, and not stir."

He looked at her, and took her hands and kissed them—but reverently—as a believer may kiss a shrine. In that moment to Flamen she was sacred; in that moment he could no more have hurt her with passion than he could have hurt her with a blow.

It was an emotion with him, and did not endure. But whilst it lasted, it was true.

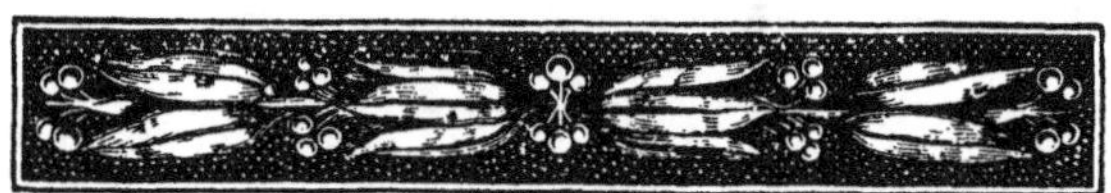

CHAPTER XVII.

THEN he took her to dine at one of the wooden cafés under the trees. There was a little sheet of water in front of it, and a gay garden around. There was a balcony and a wooden stairway; there were long trellised arbors, and little white tables, and great rose-bushes, like her own at home. They had an arbor all to themselves; a cool sweet-smelling bower of green, with a glimpse of scarlet from the flowers of some twisting beans.

They had a meal, the like of which she had never seen; such a huge melon in the centre of it, and curious wines, and coffee or cream in silver pots, or what looked like silver to her—"just like the altar-vases in the church," she said to herself.

"If only the Varnhart children were here!" she cried; but he did not echo the wish.

It was just sunset. There was a golden glow on the little bit of water. On the other side of the garden some one was playing a guitar. Under a lime-tree some girls were swinging, crying Higher! higher! at each toss.

In a longer avenue of trellised green, at a long

table, there was a noisy party of students and girls of the city; their laughter was mellowed by distance as it came over the breadth of the garden, and they sang, with fresh shrill Flemish voices, songs from an opera-bouffe of La Monnaie.

It was all pretty, and gay, and pleasant.

There was everywhere about an air of light-hearted enjoyment. Bébée sat with a wondering look in her wide-opened eyes, and all the natural instincts of her youth, that were like curled-up fruit-buds in her, unclosed softly to the light of joy.

"Is life always like this in your Rubes' land?" she asked him; that vague far-away country of which she never asked him anything more definite, and which yet was so clear before her fancy.

"Yes," he made answer to her. "Only—instead of those leaves, flowers and pomegranates; and in lieu of that tinkling guitar, a voice whose notes are esteemed like king's jewels; and in place of those little green arbors, great white palaces, cool and still, with ilex woods and orange groves and sapphire seas beyond them. Would you like to come there, Bébée?—and wear laces such as you weave, and hear singing and laughter all night long, and never work any more in the mould of the garden, or spin any more at that tiresome wheel, or go any more out in the wind, and the rain, and the winter mud to the market?"

Bébée listened, leaning her round elbows on the table, and her warm cheeks on her hands, as a child gravely listens to a fairy story. But the sumptuous picture, and the sensuous phrase he had chosen, passed by her.

It is of no use to tempt the little chaffinch of the woods with a ruby instead of a cherry. The bird is made to feed on the brown berries, on the morning dews, on the scarlet hips of roses, and the blossoms of the wind-tossed pear-boughs; the gem, though it be a monarch's, will only strike hard and tasteless on its beak.

"I would like to see it all," said Bébée, musingly trying to follow out her thoughts. "But as for the garden-work and the spinning—that I do not want to leave, because I have done it all my life; and I do not think I should care to wear lace—it would tear very soon; one would be afraid to run; and do you see I know how it is made—all that lace. I know how blind the eyes get over it, and how the hearts ache; I know how the old women starve, and the little children cry; I know that there is not a sprig of it that is not stitched with pain; the great ladies do not think, I dare say, because they have never worked at it or watched the others; but I have. And so, you see, I think if I wore it I should feel sad, and if a nail caught on it I should feel as if it were tearing the flesh of my friends. Perhaps I say it badly—but that is what I feel."

"You do not say it badly—you speak well, for you speak from the heart," he answered her, and felt a tinge of shame that he had tempted her with the gold and purple of a baser world than any that she knew.

"And yet you want to see new lands?" he pursued. "What is it you want to see there?"

"Ah, quite other things than these," cried Bébée, still leaning her cheeks on her hands. "That dancing and singing is very pretty and merry, but it is just as good when old Claude fiddles and the children skip. This wine, you tell me, is something very great—but fresh milk is much nicer, I think. It is not these kind of things I want—I want to know all about the people who lived before us; I want to know what the stars are, and what the wind is; I want to know where the lark goes when you lose him out of sight against the sun; I want to know how the old artists got to see God, that they could paint him and all his angels as they have done; I want to know how the voices got into the bells, and how they can make one's heart beat, hanging up there as they do, all alone among the jackdaws; I want to know what it is when I walk in the fields in the morning, and it is all gray and soft and still, and the corn-crake cries in the wheat, and the little mice run home to their holes, that makes me so glad and yet so sorrowful, as if I were so very near God, and yet so all alone, and such a little thing; because you see the mouse she has her hole, and the crake her own people, but I——"

Her voice faltered a little and stopped: she had never before thought out into words her own loneliness; from the long green arbor the voices of the girls and the students sang—

"Ah! le doux son d'un baiser tendre!"

Flamen was silent. The poet in him—and in an artist there is always more or less of the poet—kept him back from ridicule, nay, moved him to pity and respect.

They were absurdly simple words no doubt, had little wisdom in them, and were quite childish in their utterance, and yet they moved him curiously as a man very base and callous may at times be moved by the look in a dying deer's eyes, or by the sound of a song that some lost love once sang.

He rose and drew her hands away, and took her small face between his own hands instead.

"Poor little Bébée!" he said gently, looking down on her with a breath that was almost a sigh. "Poor little Bébée!—to envy the corn-crake and the mouse!"

She was a little startled; her cheeks grew very warm under his touch, but her eyes looked still into his without fear.

He stooped and touched her forehead with his lips, gently and without passion, almost reverently; she grew rose-hued as the bright bean-flowers, up to the light gold ripples of her hair; she trembled a little and drew back, but she was not alarmed nor yet ashamed; she was too simple of heart to feel the fear that is born of passion and of consciousness.

It was as Jeannot kissed his sister Marie, who was fifteen years old and sold milk for the Krebs people in the villages with a little green cart and a yellow dog—no more.

And yet the sunny arbor leaves and the glimpse of the blue sky swam round her indistinctly, and the sounds of the guitar grew dull upon her ear and were lost as in a rushing hiss of water, because of the great sudden unintelligible happiness that seemed to bear her little life away on it as a sea wave bears a young child off its feet.

"You do not feel alone now, Bébée?" he whispered to her.

"No!" she answered him softly under her breath, and sat still, while all her body quivered like a leaf.

No; how could she ever be alone now that this sweet, soft, unutterable touch would always be in memory upon her; how could she wish ever again now to be the corn-crake in the summer corn or the gray mouse in the hedge of hawthorn?

At that moment a student went by past the entrance of the arbor; he had a sash round his loins and a paper feather in his cap; he was playing a fife and dancing; he glanced in as he went.

"It is time to go home, Bébée," said Flamen.

CHAPTER XVIII.

SO it came to pass that Bébée's day in the big forest came and went as simply almost as any day that she had played away with the Varnhart children under the beech shadows of Cambre woods.

And when he took her to her hut at sunset before the pilgrims had returned there was a great bewildered tumult of happiness in her heart, but there was no memory with her that prevented her from looking at the shrine in the wall as she passed it, and saying with a quick gesture of the cross on brow and bosom,—

"Ah, dear Holy Mother—how good you have been! and I am back again, you see, and I will work harder than ever because of all this joy that you have given me."

And she took another moss-rose and changed it for that of the morning, which was faded, and said to Flamen,—

"Look—she sends you this. Now do you know what I mean? One is more content when She is content."

He did not answer, but he held her hands

against him a moment as they fastened in the rosebud.

"Not a word to the pilgrims, Bébée—you remember?"

"Yes, I will remember. I do not tell them every time I pray—it will be like being silent about that—it will be no more wrong than that."

But there was a touch of anxiety in the words; she was not quite certain; she wanted to be reassured. Instinct moved her not to speak of him: but habit made it seem wrong to her to have any secret from the people who had been about her from her birth.

He did not reassure her; her anxiety was pretty to watch, and he left the trouble in her heart like a bee in the chalice of a lily. Besides, the little wicket-gate was between them; he was musing whether he would push it open once more.

Her fate was in the balance, though she did not dream it: he had dealt with her tenderly, honestly, sacredly all that day—almost as much so as stupid Jeannot could have done. He had been touched by her trust in him, and by the unconscious beauty of her fancies, into a mood that was unlike all his life and habits. But after all, he said to himself—

After all!—

Where he stood in the golden evening he saw the rosy curled mouth, the soft troubled eyes, the little brown hands that still tried to fasten the rosebud, the young peach-like skin where the wind stirred the bodice;—she was only a little Flemish peasant, this poor little Bébée, a little thing of the fields and the streets, for all the dreams of God that abode with her. After all—soon or late—the end would be always the same. What matter!

She would weep a little to-morrow, and she would not kneel any more at the shrine in the garden wall; and then—and then—she would stay here and marry the good boor Jeannot, just the same after awhile; or drift away after him to Paris, and leave her two little wooden shoes, and her visions of Christ in the fields at evening, behind her for evermore, and do as all the others did, and take not only silken stockings but the Cinderella slipper that is called Gold, which brings all other good things in its train;—what matter!

He had meant this from the first, because she was so pretty, and those little wooden sabots ran so lithely over the stones; though he was not in love with her, but only idly stretched his hand for her as a child by instinct stretches to a fruit that hangs in the sun a little rosier and a little nearer than the rest.

What matter—he said to himself—she loved him, poor little soul, though she did not know it—and there would always be Jeannot glad enough of a handful of bright French gold.

He pushed the gate gently against her; her hands fastened the rosebud and drew open the latch themselves.

"Will you come in a little?" she said, with the happy light in her face. "You must not stay long, because the flowers must be watered, and then there are Annémie's patterns—they must be done or she will have no money and so no food—but if you would come in for a little? And see—if you wait a minute I will show you the roses that I shall cut to-morrow the first thing, and take down to St. Guido to Our Lady's altar in thank-offering for to-day. I should like you to choose them—you yourself—and if you would just touch them I should feel as if you gave them to her too. Will you?"

She spoke with the pretty outspoken frankness of her habitual speech, just tempered and broken with the happy, timid hesitation, the curious sense at once of closer nearness and of greater distance, that had come on her since he had kissed her among the bright bean-flowers.

He turned from her quickly.

"No, dear—no. Gather your roses alone, Bébée—if I touch them their leaves will fall."

Then, with a hurriedly backward glance down the dusky lane to see that none were looking, he bent his head and kissed her again quickly and with a sort of shame, and swung the gate behind him and went away through the boughs and the shadows.

CHAPTER XIX.

BEBEE looked after him wistfully till his figure was lost in the gloom.

The village was very quiet; a dog barking afar off and a cow lowing in the meadow were the only living things that made their presence heard; the pilgrims had not returned.

She leaned on the gate a few minutes in that indistinct, dreamy happiness which is the prerogative of innocent love.

"How wonderful it is that he should give a thought to me!" she said again and again to herself. It was as if a king had stooped for a little knot of daisied grass to set it in his crown where the great diamonds should be.

She did not reason. She did not question. She did not look beyond that hour—such is the privilege of youth.

"How I will read! How I will learn! How wise I will try to be; and how good, if I can!" she thought, swaying the little gate lightly under her weight, and looking with glad eyes at the goats as they frisked with their young in the pasture on the other side of the big trees, whilst one by one the stars came out, and an owl hooted from the palace-woods, and the frogs croaked good-nights in the rushes.

Then, like a little day-laborer as she was, with the habit of toil and the need of the poor upon her from her birth up, she shut down the latch of the gate, kissed it where his hand had rested, and went to the well to draw its nightly draught for the dry garden.

"Oh, dear roses!" she said to them as she rained the silvery showers over their nodding heads. "Oh, dear roses!—tell me—was ever anybody so happy as I am? Oh, if you say 'yes' I shall tell you you lie; silly flowers that were only born yesterday!"

But the roses shook the water off them in the wind, and said, as she wished them to say,—

"No—no one—ever before, Bébée—no one ever before."

For roses, like everything else upon earth, only speak what our own heart puts into them.

An old man went past up the lane; old Jehan, who was too ailing and aged to make one of the pilgrimage. He looked at the little quick-moving form, grayish white in the starlight, with the dark copper vessel balanced on her head, going to and fro betwixt the well and the garden.

"You did not go to the pilgrimage, poor little one!" he said across the sweet-brier hedge. "Nay, that was too bad; work, work, work—thy pretty back should not be bent double yet. You want a holiday, Bébée; well, the Fête Dieu is near. Jeannot shall take you, and maybe I can find a few sous for gingerbread and merry-go-rounds. You sit dull in the market all day; you want a feast."

Bébée colored behind the hedge, and ran in and brought three new-laid eggs that she had left in the flour-bin in the early morning, and thrust them on him through a break in the brier. It was the first time she had ever done anything of which she might not speak; she was ashamed, and yet the secret was so sweet to her.

"I am very happy, Jehan, thank God!" she murmured, with a tremulous breath and a shine in her eyes that the old man's ears and sight were too dull to discern.

"So was *she*," muttered Jehan, as he thrust the eggs into his old patched blue blouse. "So was she. And then a stumble — a blow in the lane there—a horse's kick—and all was over. All over, my pretty one—for ever and ever."

CHAPTER XX.

ON a sudden impulse Flamen, going through the woodland shadows to the city, paused and turned back; all his impulses were quick, and swayed him now hither now thither in many contrary ways.

He knew that the hour was come—that he must leave her and spare her, as to himself he phrased it, or teach her the love words that the daisies whisper to women.

And why not?—any way she would marry Jeannot.

He, half-way to the town, walked back again and paused a moment at the gate; an emotion half pitiful, half cynical, stirred in him.

Anyway he would leave her in a few days; Paris had again opened her arms to him; his old life awaited him; women who claimed him by imperious amorous demands reproached him; and after all this day he had got the Gretchen of his ideal, a great picture for the future of his fame.

As he would leave her anyway so soon, he would leave her unscathed—poor little field-flower—he could never take it with him to blossom or wither in Paris.

His world would laugh too utterly if he made for himself a mistress out of a little Fleming in two wooden shoes. Besides—

Besides, something that was half weak and half noble moved him not to lead this child, in her trust and her ignorance, into ways that when she awakened from her trance would seem to her shameful and full of sorrow. For he knew that Bébée was not as others are.

He turned back and knocked at the hut door and opened it.

Bébée was just beginning to undress herself; she had taken off her white kerchief and her wooden shoes; her pretty shoulders and her little neck shone white in the moon; her feet were bare on the mud floor.

She started with a cry and threw the handkerchief again on her shoulders, but there was no fear of him; only the unconscious instinct of her girlhood.

He thought for a moment that he would not go away until the morrow——.

"Did you want me?" said Bébée softly, with happy eyes of surprise and yet a little startled, fearing some evil might have happened to him that he should have returned thus.

"No; I do not want you, dear," he said gently; no—he did not want her, poor little soul; she wanted him, but he—there were so many of these things in his life, and he liked her too well to love her.

"No, dear, I did not want you," said Flamen, drawing her arms about him, and feeling her flutter like a little bird, while the moonlight came in through the green leaves and fell in fanciful patterns on the floor. "But I came to say—you have had one happy day, wholly happy, have you not, poor little Bébée?"

"Ah, yes!" she sighed rather than said the answer in her wondrous gladness; drawn there close to him, with the softness of his lips upon her. Could he have come back only to ask that?

"Well, that is something. You will remember it always, Bébée?" he murmured in his unconscious cruelty. "I did not wish to spoil your cloudless pleasure, dear—for you care for me a little, do you not?—so I came back to tell you only now that I go away for a little while to-morrow."

"Go away!"

She trembled in his arms and turned cold as ice; a great terror and darkness fell upon her; she had never thought that he would ever go away. He caressed her, and played with her as a boy may with a bird before he wrings its neck.

"You will come back?"

He kissed her:—"Surely."

"To-morrow?"

"Nay—not so soon."

"In a week?"

"Hardly."

"In a month, then?"

"Perhaps."

"Before winter, anyway?"

He looked aside from the beseeching, tearful, candid eyes, and kissed her hair and her throat, and said, "Yes, dear—beyond a doubt."

She clung to him, crying silently—he wished that women would not weep.

"Come, Bébée, listen," he said coaxingly, thinking to break the bitterness to her. "This is not wise, and it gives me pain. There is so much for you to do. You know so little. There is so much to learn. I will leave you many books, and you must grow quite learned in my absence. The Virgin is all very well in her way, but she cannot teach us much, poor lady. For her kingdom is called Ignorance. You must teach yourself. I leave you that to do. The days will go by quickly if you are laborious and patient. Do you love me, little one?"

For an answer she kissed his hand.

"You are a busy little Bébée always," he said, with his lips caressing her soft brown arms that were round his neck. "But you must be busier than ever whilst I am gone. So you will forget. No, no, I do not mean that:—I mean so the time will pass quickest. And I shall finish your picture, Bébée, and all Paris will see you, and the great ladies will envy the little girl with her two wooden shoes. Ah! that does not please you?—you care for none of these vanities. No. Poor little Bébée, why did God make you, or Chance breathe life into you? You are so far away from us all. It was cruel. What harm has your poor little soul ever done that, pure as a flower, it should have been sent to the hell of this world?"

She clung to him, sobbing without sound. "You will come back? You will come back?" she moaned, clasping him closer and closer.

Flamen's own eyes grew dim. But he lied to her:—"I will—I promise."

It was so much easier to say so, and it would break her sorrow. So he thought.

For the moment again he was tempted to take her with him—but, he resisted it—he would tire, and she would cling to him forever.

There was a long silence. The bleating of the little kid in the shed without was the only sound; the gray lavender blew to and fro.

Her arms were close about his throat; he kissed them again, and kissed her eyes, her cheek, her mouth; then put her from him quickly and went out.

She ran to him, and threw herself on the damp ground and held him there, and leaned her forehead on his feet. But though he looked at her with wet eyes, he did not yield, and he still said,—

"I will come back soon—very soon—be quiet, dear, let me go."

Then he kissed her once more many times, and put her gently within the door and closed it.

A low, sharp, sudden cry reached him, went to his heart, but he did not turn; he went on through the wet, green little garden, and the curling leaves, where he had found peace and had left desolation.

CHAPTER XXI.

"I WILL let her alone and she will marry Jeannot," thought Flamen; and he believed himself a good man for once in his life, and pitied himself for having become a sentimentalist.

She would marry Jeannot, and bear many children, as those people always did; and ruddy little peasants would cling about those pretty, soft, little breasts of hers; and she would love them after the manner of such women, and be very content clattering over the stones in her wooden shoes; and growing brown and stout, and more careful after money, and ceasing to dream of unknown things, and not seeing God at all in the fields, but looking low and beholding only the ears of the gleaning wheat and the feet of the tottering children; and so gaining her bread, and losing her soul, and stooping nearer and nearer to earth till she dropped into it like one of her own wind-blown wall-flowers when the bee has sucked out all its sweetness and the heats have scorched up all its bloom:—yes, of course, she would marry Jeannot and end so!

Meanwhile he had his Gretchen, and that was the one great matter.

So he left the street of Mary of Burgundy, and went on his way out of the chiming city as its matin bells were rung, and took with him a certain regret, and the only innocent affection that had ever awakened in him; and thought of his self-negation with half admiration and half derision; and so drifted away into the whirlpool of his amorous, cynical, changeful, passionate, callous, many-colored life, and said to himself as he saw the last line of the low green plains shine against the sun,—"She will marry Jeannot—of course, she will marry Jeannot. And my Gretchen is greater than Scheffer's."

What else mattered very much, after all, except what they would say in Paris of Gretchen?

CHAPTER XXII.

PEOPLE saw that Bébée had grown very quiet. But that was all they saw.

Her little face was pale as she sat among her glowing autumn blossoms, by the side of the cobbler's stall; and when the Varnhart children cried at the gate to her to come and play, she would answer gently that she was too busy to have play-time now.

The fruit-girl of the Montagne de la Cour hooted after her, "Gone so soon?—oh hé! what did I say?—a fine pine is sugar in the teeth a second only, but the brown nuts you may crack all the seasons round. Well, did you make good harvest while it lasted? has Jeannot a fat bridal portion promised?"

And old Jehan, who was the tenderest soul of them all in the lane by the swans' water, would come and look at her wistfully as she worked among the flowers, and would say to her,—

"Dear little one, there is some trouble—does it come of that painted picture? You never laugh now, Bébée, and that is bad. A girl's laugh is pretty to hear; my girl laughed like little bells ringing—and then it stopped, all at once; they said she was dead. But you are not dead, Bébée. And yet you are so silent; one would say you were."

But to the mocking of the fruit-girl, as to the tenderness of old Jehan, Bébée answered nothing; the lines of her pretty curled mouth grew grave and sad, and in her eyes there was a wistful bewildered pathetic appeal like the look in the eyes of a beaten dog, which, while it aches with pain, does not cease to love its master.

One resolve upheld her, and made her feet firm on the stones of the streets and her lips mute under all they said to her. She would learn all she could, and be good, and patient, and wise, if trying could make her wise, and so do his will in all things—until he should come back.

"You are not gay, Bébée," said Annémie, who grew so blind that she could scarce see the flags at the mastheads, and who still thought that she pricked the lace patterns and earned her bread.

"You are not gay, dear. Has any lad gone to sea that your heart goes away with, and do you watch for his ship coming in with the coasters? It is weary work waiting—but it is all the men think us fit for, child. They may set sail as they like; every new port has new faces for them; but we are to sit still and to pray if we like, and never murmur, be the voyage ever so long, but be ready with a smile and a kiss, a fresh pipe of tobacco, and a dry pair of socks;—that is a man. We may have cried our hearts out—we must have ready the pipe and the socks, or, 'Is that what you call love?' they grumble. You want mortal patience if you love a man,—it is like a fretful child that thumps you when your breast is bare to it. Still—be you patient, dear, just as I am, just as I am."

And Bébée would shudder as she swept the cobwebs from the garret walls,—patient as she was—she who had sat here fifty years watching for a dead man and for a wrecked ship.

CHAPTER XXIII.

THE wheat was reapen in the fields, and the brown earth turned afresh. The white and purple chrysanthemums bloomed against the flowerless rose-bushes, and the little gray Michaelmas daisy flourished where the dead carnations had spread their glories. Leaves began to fall and chilly winds to sigh among the willows; the squirrels began to store away their nuts, and the poor to pick up the broken, bare boughs.

"He said he would come before winter," thought Bébée, every day when she rose and felt each morning cooler and grayer than the one before it; winter was near.

Her little feet already were cold in their wooden shoes; and the robin already sang in the twigs of the sear sweet-brier; but she had the brave sweet faith which nothing kills, and she did not doubt—oh! no, she did not doubt, she was only tired.

Tired of the strange, sleepless, feverish nights; tired of the long, dull, empty days; tired of watching down the barren, leafless lane; tired of hearkening breathless to each step on the rustling dead leaves; tired of looking always, always, always, into the ruddy autumn evenings and the cold autumn starlight, and never hearing what she listened for, never seeing what she sought; tired as a child may be, lost in a wood, and wearily wearing its small strength and breaking its young heart in search of the track forever missed, of the home forever beyond the horizon.

Still she did her work and kept her courage.

She took her way into the town with her basket full of the ruby and amber of the dusky autumn blossoms, and when those failed, and the garden was quite desolate, except for a promise of haws and of holly, she went, as she had always done, to the lace-room, and gained her bread and the chickens' corn each day by winding the thread round the bobbins; and at nightfall, when she had plodded home through the darksome roads and over the sodden turf, and had lit her rushlight and sat down to her books, with her hand buried in her hair, and her eyes smarting from the strain of the lace-work, and her heart aching with that new and deadly pain which never left her now, she would read—read—read—read, and try and store her brain with knowledge, and try and grasp these vast new meanings of life that the books opened to her, and try and grow less ignorant against he should return.

There was much she could not understand, but there was also much she could.

Her mind was delicate and quick, her intelligence swift and strong; she bought old books at bookstalls with pence that she saved by going without her dinner. The keeper of the stall, a shrewd old soul, explained some hard points to her, and chose good volumes for her, and lent others to this solitary little student in her wooden shoes and with her pale child's face.

So she toiled hard and learned much, and grew taller and very thin, and got a look in her eyes like a lost dog's, and yet never lost heart or wandered in the task that he had set her, or in her faith in his return.

"Burn the books, Bébée," whispered the children again and again, clinging to her skirts. "Burn the wicked, silent things. Since you have had them you never sing, or romp, or laugh, and you look so white—so white."

Bébée kissed them, but kept to her books.

Jeannot going by from the forest night after night saw the light twinkling in the hut window, and sometimes crept softly up and looked through the chinks of the wooden shutter, and saw her leaning over some big old volume with her pretty brows drawn together, and her mouth shut close in earnest effort, and he would curse the man who had changed her so, and go away with rage in his breast and tears in his eyes, not daring to say any thing, but knowing that never would Bébée's little brown hand lie in love within his own.

Nor even in friendship, for he had rashly spoken rough words against the stranger from Rubes' land, and Bébée ever since then had passed him by with a grave simple greeting, and when he had brought her in timid gifts a barrow-load of fagots, had thanked him, but had bidden him take the wood home to his mother.

"You think evil things of me, Bébée?" good Jeannot had pleaded, with a sob in his voice; and she had answered gently,—

"No; but do not speak to me, that is all."

Then he had cursed her absent lover, and Bébée gone within and closed her door.

She had no idea that the people thought ill of her. They were cold to her, and such coldness made her heart ache a little more. But the one great love in her possessed her so strongly that all other things were half unreal.

She did her daily housework from sheer habit, and she studied because he had told her to do it, and because with the sweet, stubborn, credulous faith of her youth, she never doubted that he would return.

Otherwise there was no perception of real life in her; she dreamed and prayed, and prayed and dreamed, and never ceased to do either one or the other, even when she was scattering potato-peels to the fowls, or shaking carrots loose of the soil, or sweeping the snow from her hut door, or going out in the raw dark dawn as the single little sad bell of St. Guido tolled through the stillness for the first mass.

For though even Father Francis looked angered

at her because he thought she was stubborn, and hid some truth and some shame from him at confession, yet she went resolutely and oftener than ever to kneel in the dusty, dusky, crumbling old church, for it was all she could do for him who was absent—so she thought—and she did not feel quite so far away from him when she was beseeching Christ to have care of his soul and of his body.

All her pretty dreams were dead.

She never heard any story in the robin's song, or saw any promise in the sunset clouds, or fancied that angels came about her in the night—never now.

The fields were gray and sad; the birds were little brown things; the stars were cold and far off; the people she had used to care for were like mere shadows that went by her meaningless and without interest, and all she thought of was the one step that never came; all she wanted was the one touch she never felt.

"You have done wrong, Bébée, and you will not own it," said the few neighbors who ever spoke to her.

Bébée looked at them with wistful, uncomprehending eyes.

"I have done no wrong," she said gently, but no one believed her.

A girl did not shut herself up and wane pale and thin for nothing, so they reasoned. She might have sinned as she had liked if she had been sensible after it, and married Jeannot.

But to fret mutely, and shut her lips, and seem as though she had done nothing—that was guilt indeed.

For her village, in its small way, thought as the big world thinks.

CHAPTER XXIV.

FULL winter came.

The snow was deep, and the winds drove the people with whips of ice along the dreary country roads and the steep streets of the city. The bells of the dogs and the mules sounded sadly through the white misty silence of the Flemish plains, and the weary horses slipped and fell on the frozen ruts and on the jagged stones in the little frost-shut Flemish towns. Still the Flemish folk were gay enough in many places.

There were fairs and kermesses; there were puppet-plays and church-feasts; there were sledges on the plains and skates on the canals; there were warm woolen hoods and ruddy wood-fires; there were tales of demons and saints, and bowls of hot onion soup; sugar images for the little children, and blessed beads for the maidens clasped on rosy throats with lovers' kisses; and in the city itself there was the high tide of the winter pomp and mirth, with festal scenes in the churches, and balls at the palaces, and all manner of gay things in toys and jewels, and music playing cheerily under the leafless trees, and flashes of scarlet cloth, and shining furs, and happy faces, and golden curls, in the carriages that climbed the Montagne de la Cour, and filled the big place around the statue of stout Godfrey.

In the little village above St. Guido, Bébée's neighbors were merry too, in their simple way.

The women worked away wearily at their lace in the dim winter light, and made a wretched living by it, but all the same they got penny playthings for their babies, and a bit of cake for their Sunday hearth. They drew together in homely and cordial friendship, and of an afternoon when dusk fell wove their lace in company in Mère Krebs's mill-house kitchen, with the children and the dogs at their feet on the bricks, so that one big fire might serve for all, and all be lighted with one big rush candle, and all be beguiled by chit-chat and songs, stories of spirits, and whispers of ghosts, and now and then when the wind howled at its worst, a paternoster or two said in common for the men toiling in the barges or drifting up the Scheldt.

In these gatherings Bébée's face was missed, and the blithe soft sound of her voice, like a young thrush singing, was never heard.

The people looked in, and saw her sitting over a great open book—often her hearth had no fire.

Then the children grew tired of asking her to play; and their elders began to shake their heads; she was so pale and so quiet, there must be some evil in it—so they began to think.

Little by little people dropped away from her.

Who knew, the gossips said, what shame or sin the child might not have on her sick little soul?

True, Bébée worked hard just the same, and just the same was seen trudging to and fro in the dusk of dawns and afternoons in her two little wooden shoes. She was gentle and laborious, and gave the children her goat's milk, and the old women the brambles of her garden.

But they grew afraid of her—afraid of that sad, changeless, far-away look in her eyes, and of the mute weariness that was on her—and, being perplexed, were sure, like all ignorant creatures, that what was secret must be also vile.

So they hung aloof, and let her alone, and by-and-by scarcely nodded as they passed her, but said to Jeannot,—

"You were spared a bad thing, lad; the child was that grand painter's light-o'-love, that is plain to see. The mischief all comes of the stuff old Antoine filled her head with—a stray little by-blow of chickweed that he cockered up like a rare carnation. Oh! do not fly in a rage, Jeannot; the child is no good, and would have made an honest man rue. Take heart of grace, and praise the saints, and marry Katto's Lisa."

But Jeannot would never listen to the slanderers, and would never look at Lisa, even though the door of the little hut was always closed against him, and whenever he met Bébée on the highway she never seemed to see him more than she saw the snow that her sabots were treading.

One night in the midwinter-time old Annémie died.

Bébée found her in the twilight with her head against the garret window, and her left side all shriveled and useless. She had a little sense left, and a few fleeting breaths to draw.

"Look for the brig," she muttered. "You will not see the flag at the masthead for the fog to-night; but his socks are dry and his pipe is ready. Keep looking—keep looking—she will be in port to-night."

But her dead sailor never came into port; she went to him. The poor, weakened, faithful old body of her was laid in the graveyard of the poor, and the ships came and went under the empty garret window, and Bébée was all alone.

She had no more anything to work for, or any bond with the lives of others. She could live on the roots of her garden and the sale of her hens' eggs, and she could change the turnips and carrots that grew in a little strip of her ground for the quantity of bread that she needed.

So she gave herself up to the books, and drew herself more and more within from the outer world. She did not know that the neighbors thought very evil of her; she had only one idea in her mind—to be more worthy of him against he should return.

The winter passed away somehow; she did not know how.

It was a long, cold, white blank of frozen

silence; that was all. She studied hard, and had got a quaint, strange, deep, scattered knowledge out of her old books; her face had lost all its roundness and color, but, instead, the forehead had gained breadth and the eyes had the dim fire of a student's.

Every night when she shut her volumes she thought,—

"I am a little nearer him. I know a little more."

Just so every morning, when she bathed her hands in the chilly water, she thought to herself, "I will make my skin as soft as I can for him, that it may be like the ladies' he has loved."

Love to be perfect must be a religion, as well as a passion. Bébée's was so. Like George Herbert's serving-maiden, she swept no specks of dirt away from a floor without doing it to the service of her lord.

Only Bébée's lord was a king of earth, made of earth's dust and vanities.

But what did she know of that?

CHAPTER XXV.

THE winter went by, and the snow-drops and crocus and pale hepatica smiled at her from the black clods. Every other spring-time Bébée had run with fleet feet under the budding trees down into the city, and had sold sweet little wet bunches of violets and brier before all the snow was melted from the eaves of the Broodhuis.

"The winter is gône," the townspeople used to say; "look, there is Bébée with the flowers."

But this year they did not see the little figure itself like a rosy crocus standing against the brown timbers of the Maison de Roi.

Bébée had not heart to pluck a single blossom of them all. She let them all live, and tended them so that the little garden should look its best and brightest to him when his hand should lift its latch.

Only he was so long coming—so very long; the violets died away, and the first rosebuds came in their stead, and still Bébée looked every dawn and every nightfall vainly down the empty road.

Nothing kills young creatures like the bitterness of waiting.

Pain they will bear, and privation they will pass through, fire and water and storm will not appal them, nor wrath of heaven and earth, but waiting—the long, tedious, sickly, friendless days, that drop one by one in their eternal sameness into the weary past, these kill slowly but surely, as the slow dropping of water frets away rock.

The summer came.

Nearly a year had gone by. Bébée worked early and late. The garden bloomed like one big rose, and the neighbors shook their heads to see the flowers blossom and fall without bringing in a single coin.

She herself spoke less seldom than ever, and now when old Jehan, who never had understood the evil thoughts of his neighbors, asked her what ailed her that she looked so pale and never stirred down to the city, now her courage failed her, and the tears brimmed over her eyes, and she could not call up a brave brief word to answer him. For the time was so long, and she was so tired.

Still she never doubted that her lover would come back: he had said he would come: she was as sure that he would come as she was sure that God came in the midst of the people when the silver bell rang and the Host was borne by on high.

Bébée did not heed much, but she vaguely felt the isolation she was left in: as a child too young to reason feels cold and feels hunger.

"No one wants me here now that Annémie is

gone," she thought to herself, as the sweet green spring days unfolded themselves one by one like the buds of the brier-rose hedges.

And now and then even the loyal little soul of her gave way, and sobbing on her lonely bed in the long dark nights, she would cry out against him, "Oh, why not have left me alone? I was so happy—so happy!"

And then she would reproach herself with treason to him and ingratitude, and hate herself and feel guilty in her own sight to have thus sinned against him in thought for one single instant.

For there are natures in which the generosity of love is so strong that it feels its own just pain to be disloyalty; and Bébée's was one of them. And if he had killed her she would have died hoping only that no moan had escaped her under the blow that ever could accuse him.

These natures, utterly innocent by force of self-accusation and self-abasement, suffer at once the torment of the victim and the criminal.

CHAPTER XXVI.

ONE day in the May weather she sat within-doors with a great book upon her table, but no sight for it in her aching eyes. The starling hopped to and fro on the sunny floor; the bees boomed in the porch; the tinkle of sheep's bells came in on the stillness. All was peaceful and happy except the little weary, breaking, desolate heart that beat in her like a caged bird's.

"He will come; I am sure he will come," she said to herself; but she was so tired, and it was so long—oh, dear God!—so very long.

A hand tapped at the lattice. The shrill voice of Reine, the sabot-maker's wife, broken with anguish, called through the hanging ivy,—

"Bébée, you are a wicked one, they say, but the only one there is at home in the village this day. Get you to town for the love of Heaven, and send Doctor Max hither, for my pet, my flower, my child lies dying, and not a soul near, and she black as a coal with choking—go, go, go!—and Mary will forgive you your sins. Save the little one, dear Bébée, do you hear? and I will pray God and speak fair the neighbors for you. Go!"

Bébée rose up, startled by the now unfamiliar sound of a human voice, and looked at the breathless mother with eyes of pitying wonder.

"Surely I will go," she said, gently; "but there is no need to bribe me. I have not sinned greatly —that I know."

Then she went out quickly and ran through the lanes and into the city for the sick child, and found the wise man, and sent him, and did the errand rather in a sort of sorrowful sympathetic instinct than in any reasoning consciousness of doing good.

When she was moving through the once-familiar and happy ways as the sun was setting on the golden fronts of the old houses, and the chimes were ringing from the many towers, a strange sense of unreality, of non-existence, fell upon her.

Could it be she?—she indeed—who had gone there the year before the gladdest thing that the earth bore, with no care except to shelter her flowers from the wind, and keep the freshest blossoms for the burgomaster's housewife?

She did not think thus to herself; but a vague doubt that she could ever have been the little gay, laborious, happy Bébée, with troops of friends and endless joys for every day that dawned, came over her as she went by the black front of the Broodhuis.

The strong voice of Lisa, the fruit-girl, jarred on her as she passed the stall under its yellow awning that was flapping sullenly in the evening wind.

"Oh hé, little fool," the mocking voice cried, "the rind of the fine pine is full of prickles, and stings the lips when the taste is gone?—to be sure —crack common nuts like me, and you are never wanting—hazels grow free in every copse. Prut, tut! your grand lover lies a-dying; so the students read out of this just now; and you such a simpleton as not to get a roll of napoleons out of him before he went to rot in Paris. I dare say he was poor as sparrows, if one knew the truth. He was only a painter after all."

Lisa tossed her as she spoke a torn sheet, in which she was wrapping gentians: it was a piece of newspaper some three weeks old, and in it there was a single line or so which said that the artist Flamen, whose Gretchen was the wonder of the Salon of the year, lay sick unto death in his rooms in Paris.

Bébée stood and read; the strong ruddy western light upon the type, the taunting laughter of the fruit-girl on her ear.

A bitter shriek rang from her that made even the cruelty of Lisa's mirth stop in a sudden terror.

She stood staring like a thing changed to stone down on the one name that to her filled all the universe.

"Ill—he is ill—do you hear?" she echoed piteously, looking at Lisa; "and you say he is poor?"

"Poor? for sure! is he not a painter?" said the fruit-girl, roughly. She judged by her own penniless student-lads; and she was angered with herself for feeling sorrow for this little silly thing that she had loved to torture.

"You have been bad and base to me; but now —I bless you, I love you, I will pray for you," said Bébée, in a swift broken breath, and with a look upon her face that startled into pain her callous enemy.

Then without another word, she thrust the paper in her bosom, and ran out of the square breathless with haste and with a great resolve.

He was ill—and he was poor! The brave little soul of her leaped at once to action. He was sick, and far away; and poor they said. All danger and all difficulty faded to nothing before the vision of his need.

Bébée was only a little foundling who ran about in wooden shoes; but she had the "dog's soul" in her—the soul that will follow faithfully though to receive a curse, that will defend loyally though to meet a blow, and that will die mutely loving to the last.

She went home, how she never knew; and without the delay of a moment packed up a change of linen, and fed the fowls and took the key of the hut down to old Jehan's cabin. The old man was only half-witted by reason of his affliction for his dead daughter, but he was shrewd enough to understand what she wanted of him, and honest enough to do it.

"I am going into the city," she said to him; "and if I am not back to-night, will you feed the starling and the hens, and water the flowers for me?"

Old Jehan put his head out of his lattice; it was seven in the evening, and he was going to bed.

"What are you after, little one?" he asked; "going to show the fine buckles at a students' ball? Nay, fie—that is not like you."

"I am going to—pray,—dear Jehan," she answered, with a sob in her throat and the first falsehood she ever had told. "Do what I ask you—do for your dead daughter's sake—or the birds and the flowers will die of hunger and thirst. Take the key and promise me."

He took the key, and promised.

"Do not let them see those buckles shine; they will rob you," he added.

Bébée ran from him fast; every moment that was lost was so precious and so terrible. To pause a second for fear's sake never occurred to her. She went forth as fearlessly as a young swallow, born in northern April days, flies forth on instinct to new lands and over unknown seas when autumn falls.

Necessity and action breathed new life into her. The hardy and brave peasant ways of her were awoke once more. She had been strong to wait silently with the young life in her dying out drop by drop in the heart-sickness of long delay. She was strong now to throw herself into strange countries and dim perils and immeasurable miseries, on the sole chance that she might be of service to him.

A few human souls here and there can love like dogs. Bébée's was one.

CHAPTER XXVII.

IT was dark. The May days are short in the north lands of the Scheldt.

She had her little winter cloak of frieze and her wooden shoes and her little white cap, with the sunny curls rippling out of it in their pretty rebellion. She had her little lantern too; and her bundle; and she had put a few fresh eggs in her basket, with some sweet herbs and the palm-sheaf that Father Francis had blessed last Easter—for who could tell, she thought, how ill he might not be, or how poor?

She hardly gave a look to the hut as she ran by its garden gate; all her heart was on in front, in the vague far-off country where he lay sick unto death.

She ran fast through the familiar lanes into the city. She was not very sure where Paris was, but she had the name clear and firm, and she knew that people were always coming and going thence and thither, so that she had no fear she should not find it.

She went straight to the big busy bewildering place in the Leopold quarter where the iron horses fumed every day and night along the iron ways. She had never been there before, but she knew it was by that great highway that the traffic to Paris was carried on, and she knew that it would carry people also as well.

There were bells clanging, lights flashing, and crowds pushing and shouting, as she ran up—a little gray figure, with the lantern-spark glimmering like any tiny glow-worm astray in a gas-lit city.

"To Paris?" she asked, entreatingly, going where she saw others going, to a little grated wicket in a wall.

"Twenty-seven francs—quick!" they demanded of her.

Bébée gave a great cry, and stood still, trembling and trying not to sob aloud. She had never thought of money; she had forgotten that youth and strength and love and willing feet and piteous prayers—all went for nothing as this world is made.

A hope flashed on her, and a glad thought. She loosed the silver buckles, and held them out.

"Would you take these? They are worth much more."

There was a derisive laughter; some one bade here with an oath begone; rough shoulders jostled her away. She stretched her arms out piteously.

"Take me—oh, pray take me! I will go with the sheep, with the cattle—only, only, take me!"

But in the rush and roar none heeded her; some thief snatched the silver buckles from her hand, and made off with them and was lost in the throng; a great iron beast rushed by her, snorting flame and bellowing smoke; there was a roll like thunder, and all was dark; the night express had passed on its way to Paris.

Bébée stood still, crushed for a moment with the noise and the cruelty and the sense of absolute desolation; she scarcely noticed that the buckles had been stolen; she had only one thought—to get to Paris.

"Can I never-go without money?" she asked at the wicket; the man there glanced a moment, with a touch of pity, at the little wistful face.

"The least is twenty francs—surely you must know that?" he said, and shut his grating with a clang.

Bébée turned away and went out of the great cruel tumultuous place; her heart ached and her brain was giddy, but the sturdy courage of her nature rose to need.

"There is no way at all to go without money to Paris, I suppose?" she asked of an old woman whom she knew a little, who sold nuts and little pictures of saints and wooden playthings under the trees, in the avenue hard by.

The old woman shook her head.

"Eh?—no, dear. There is nothing to be done anywhere in the world without money. Look, I cannot get a litre of nuts to sell unless I pay beforehand."

"Would it be far to walk?"

"Far! Holy Jesus! It is right away in the heart

of France — over two hundred miles, they say; straight out through the forest. Not but what my son did walk it once—and he a shoemaker, who knows what walking costs; and he is well-to-do there now—not that he ever writes. When they want nothing people never write."

"And he walked into Paris?"

"Yes, ten years ago. He had nothing but a few sous and an ash stick, and he had a fancy to try his luck there. And after all our feet were given us to travel with. If you go there and you see him, tell him to send me something—I am tired of selling nuts."

Bébée said nothing, but went on her road; since there was no other way but to walk she would take that way; the distance and the hardship did not appal two little feet that were used to traverse so many miles of sun-baked summer dust and of frozen winter mud unblenchingly year after year.

The time it would take made her heart sink indeed. He was ill. God knew what might happen. But neither the length of leagues nor the fatigue of body daunted her. She only saw his eyes dim with pain and his lips burned with fever.

She would walk twenty miles a day, and then, perhaps, she might get lifts here and there on hay-wagons or in peddlers' carts; people had always used to be kind to her. Anyhow she counted she might reach Paris well in fifteen days.

She sat under a shrine in a by street a moment, and counted the copper pieces she had on her;

they were few, and the poor pretty buckles that she might have sold to get money, were stolen.

She had some twenty sous and a dozen eggs; she thought she might live on that; she had wanted to take the eggs to him, but after all, to keep life in her until she could reach Paris was the one great thing.

"What a blessing it is to have been born poor; and to have lived hardly—one wants so little!" she thought to herself.

Then she put up the sous in the linen bosom of her gown, and trimmed her little lantern and knelt down in the quiet darkness and prayed a moment, with the hot agonized tears rolling down her face, and then rose and stepped out bravely in the cool of the night, on the great southwest road towards Paris.

The thought never once crossed her to turn back, and go again into the shelter of her own little hut among the flowers. He was sick there, dying, for anything she knew—that was the only thing she remembered.

It was a clear, starlit night, and everywhere the fragrance of the spring was borne in from the wide green plains, and the streams where the rushes were blowing.

She walked ten miles easily, the beautiful gray shadow all about her. She had never been so far from home in all her life, except to that one Kermesse at Mechlin. But she was not afraid.

With the movement, and the air, and the sense

that she was going to him, which made her happy even in her misery, something of the old, sweet, lost fancies came to her.

She smiled at the stars through her tears, and as the poplars swayed and murmured in the wind, they looked to her like the wings and the swords of a host of angels.

Her way lay out through the forest, and in that sweet green woodland she was not afraid—no more afraid than the fawns were.

At Boitsfort she shrank a little, indeed. Here there were the open-air restaurants, and the café gardens all alight for the pleasure-seekers from the city; here there were music and laughter, and horses with brass bells, and bright colors on high in the wooden balconies, and below among the blossoming hawthorn hedges. She had to go through it all, and she shuddered a little as she ran, thinking of that one priceless, deathless forest day when he had kissed her first.

But the pleasure-people were all busied with their mirth and mischief, and took no notice of the little gray figure in the starry night. She went on along the grassy roads, under the high arching trees, with the hoot of the owls and the cry of the rabbits on the stillness.

At Groenendael, in the heart of the forest, midnight was striking as she entered the village. Every one was asleep. The lights were all out. The old ruined priory frowned dark under the clouds.

She shivered a little again, and began to feel chill and tired, yet did not dare to knock at any one of the closed house-doors—she had no money.

So she walked on her first ten unknown miles, meeting a few people only, and being altogether unmolested—a small gray figure, trotting in two little wooden shoes.

They thought her a peasant going to a fair or a lace-mill, and no one did her more harm than to wish her good-night in rough Flemish.

When the dawn began to whiten above the plains of the east, she saw an empty cowshed filled with hay; she was a little tired, and lay down and rested an hour or two, as a young lamb might have lain on the dried clover, for she knew that she must keep her strength and husband her power, or never reach across the dreary length of the foreign land to Paris.

But by full sunrise she was on her way again, bathing her face in a brook and buying a sou's worth of bread and flet-milk at the first cottage that she passed in bright, leaf-bowered Hoeylaert.

The forest was still all around her, with its exquisite life of bough and blossom, and murmur of insect and of bird. She told her beads, praying as she went, and was almost happy.

God would not let him die. Oh, no, not till she had kissed him once more, and could die with him.

The hares ran across the path, and the blue butterflies flew above-head. There was purple gloom of pinewood, and sparkling verdure of aspen and elm. There were distant church carillons ringing, and straight golden shafts of sunshine streaming.

She was quite sure God would not let him die.

She hoped that he might be very poor. At times he had talked as if he were, and then she might be of so much use. She knew how to deal with fever and suffering. She had sat up many a night with the children of the village. The gray sisters had taught her many of their ways of battling with disease; and she could make fresh cool drinks, and she could brew beautiful remedies from simple herbs. There was so much that she might do; her fancy played with it almost happily. And then, only to touch his hand, only to hear his voice; her heart rose at the thought, as a lark to its morning song.

At Rixensart, buried in its greenery, as she went through it in morning light, some peasants greeted her cheerily, and called to her to rest in a house-porch, and gave her honey and bread. She could not eat much; her tongue was parched and her throat was dry, but the kindness was precious to her, and she went on her road the stronger for it.

"It is a long way to walk to Paris," said the woman, with some curious wonder. Bébée smiled, though her eyes grew wet.

"She has the look of the little Gesù," said the Rixensart people, and they watched her away with a vague timid pity.

So she went on through Ottignies and La Roche, to Villers, and left the great woods and the city chimes behind her, and came through the green abbey valleys through Tilly and Ligny, and Fleurus, and so into the coal and iron fields that lie round Charleroi.

Here her heart grew sick, and her courage sank under the noise and the haste, before the blackness and the hideousness. She had never seen anything like it. She thought it was hell, with the naked, swearing, fighting people, and the red fires leaping night and day. Nevertheless, if hell it were, since it lay betwixt her and him, she found force to brave and cross it.

The miners and glass-blowers and nail-makers, rough and fierce and hard, frightened her. The women did not look like women, and the children ran and yelled at her, and set their dogs upon her. The soil was thick with dust like soot, and the trees were seared and brown. There was no peace in the place, and no loveliness. Eighty thousand folks toiled together in the hopeless Tophet, and swarmed, and struggled, and labored, and multiplied, in joyless and endless wrestling against hunger and death.

She got through it somehow, hiding often from the ferocious youngsters, and going sleepless rather than lie in those dens of filth; but she seemed so many, many years older when Charleroi lay at last behind her—so many, many years older than when she had sat and spun in the garden at home.

When she was once in the valley of the Sambre she was more herself again, only she felt weaker than she had ever done, because she only dared to spend one of her sous each day, and one sou got so little food.

In the woods and fields about Alne she began to breathe again, like a bird loosed to the air after being shut in a wooden trap. Green corn, green boughs, green turf, mellow chimes of church-bells, humming of golden bees, cradle songs of women spinning, homely odors of little herb-gardens and of orchard-trees under cottage walls—these had been around her all her life; she only breathed freely among them.

She often felt tired, and her wooden shoes were wearing so thin that the hot dust of the road at noonday burnt her feet through them. Sometimes, too, she felt a curious brief faintness such as she had never known, for the lack of food and the long fatigue began to tell even on her hardy little body.

But she went on bravely, rarely doing less than her twenty miles a day, and sometimes more, walking often in the night to save time, and lying down in cow-sheds or under haystacks in the noontide.

For the most part people were kind to her; they saw she was so very young and so poor.

Women would give her leave to bathe herself in their bed-chambers, and children would ask her to wait on the village bench under the chestnut-tree, while they brought her their pet lamb or their tumbler pigeons to look at, but, for the most part—unless she was very, very tired—she would not wait. It took her so long, and who could tell how it fared with him in Paris?

Into the little churches, scattered over the wide countries between Charleroi and Erquelinnes, she would turn aside, indeed; but, then, that was only to say a prayer for him; that was not loss to him, but gain.

So she walked on until she reached the frontier of France. She began to get a little giddy; she began to see the blue sky and the green level always swirling round her as if some one were spinning them to frighten her, but still she would not be afraid; she went on, and on, and on, till she set her last step on the soil of Flanders.

Here a new strange, terrible, incomprehensible obstacle opposed her: she had no papers; they thrust her back and spoke to her as if she were a criminal. She could not understand what they could mean. She had never heard of these laws and rules. She vaguely comprehended that she must not enter France, and stunned and heart-broken she dropped down under a tree, and for the first time sobbed as if her very life would weep itself away.

She could see nothing, understand nothing. There were the same road, the same hedges, the same fields, the same white cottages, and peasants in blue shirts and dun-hued oxen in the wagons. She saw no mark, no difference, ere they told her where she stood was Belgium, and where they stood was France, and that she must not pass from one into the other.

The men took no notice of her. They went

back into their guard-house, and smoked and drank. A cat sunned herself under a scarlet bean. The white clouds sailed on before a southerly sky. She might die here—he there—and nothing seemed to care.

After awhile an old hawker came up; he was traveling with wooden clocks from the Black Forest. He stopped and looked at her, and asked her what she ailed.

She knelt down at his feet in the dust.

"Oh, help me!" she cried to him. "Oh, pray, help me! I have walked all the way from Brussels—that is my country, and now they will not let me pass that house where the soldiers are. They say I have no papers. What papers should I have? I do not know. When one has done no harm, and does not owe a sou anywhere, and has walked all the way—Is it money that they want? I have none; and they stole my silver clasps in Brussels; and if I do not get to Paris I must die—die without seeing him again—ever again, dear God!"

She dropped her head upon the dust and crouched and sobbed there, her courage broken by this new barrier that she had never dreamed would come between herself and Paris.

The old hawker looked at her thoughtfully. He had seen much of men and women, and knew truth from counterfeit, and he was moved by the child's agony.

He stooped and whispered in her ear,—

"Get up quick, and I will pass you. It is against

the law, and I may go to prison for it. Never mind; one must risk something in this world, or else be a cur. My daughter has stayed behind in Marbais sweethearting; her name is on my passport, and her age and face will do for yours. Get up and follow me close, and I will get you through. Poor little soul! whatever your woe is it is real enough, and you are such a young and pretty thing. Get up, the guards are in their house, they have not seen; follow me, and you must not speak a word; they must take you for a German, dumb as wood."

She got up and obeyed him, not comprehending, but only vaguely seeing that he was friendly to her, and would pass her over into France.

The old man made a little comedy at the barrier, and scolded her as though she were his daughter for losing her way as she came to meet him, and then crying like a baby.

The guards looked at her carelessly, joked the hawker on her pretty face, looked the papers over, and let her through, believing her the child of the clock-maker of the Hartz. Some lies are blessed as truth.

"I have done wrong in the law, but not before God, I think, little one," said the peddler. "Nay —do not thank me, or go on like that; we are in sight of the customs men still, and if they suspected, it would be the four walls of a cell only that you and I should see to-night. And now tell me your story, poor maiden—why are you on foot through a strange country?"

But Bébée would not tell him her story; she was confused and dazed still. She did not know rightly what had happened to her; but she could not talk of herself, nor of why she traveled thus to Paris.

The old hawker got cross at her silence, and called her an unthankful jade, and wished that he had left her to her fate, and parted company with her at two cross-roads, saying his path did not lie with hers; and then when he had done that, was sorry, and being a tender-hearted soul, hobbled back, and would fain press a five-franc piece on her; and Bébée, refusing it all the while, kissed his old brown hands and blessed him, and broke away from him, and so went on again solitary towards St. Quentin.

The country was very flat and poor, and yet the plains had a likeness in them to her own wide Brabant downs, where the tall green wheat was blowing and the barges dropping down the sluggish streams.

She was very footsore; very weary; very hungry so often; but she was in France—in his country;—and her spirit rose with the sense of that nearness to him.

After all God was so good to her; there were fine bright days and nights; a few showers had fallen, but merely passing ones; the air was so cool and so balmy that it served her almost as food; and she seldom found people so unkind that they refused for her single little sou to give her a crust of bread and let her lie in an outhouse.

After all God was very good; and by the sixteenth or seventeenth day she would be in the city of Paris.

She was a little light-headed at times from insufficient nourishment; especially after waking from strange dreams in unfamiliar places; sometimes the soil felt tremulous under her, and the sky spun round; but she struggled against the feeling, and kept a brave heart, and tried to be afraid of nothing.

Sometimes at night she thought she saw old Annémie. "But what if I do?" she said to herself; "Annémie never will hurt me."

And now, as she grew nearer her goal, her natural buoyancy of spirit returned as it had never done to her since the evening that he had kissed and left her. As her body grew lighter and more exhausted, her fancy grew keener and more dominant. All things of the earth and air spoke to her as she went along as they had used to do. All that she had learned from the books in the long cold months came to her clear and wonderful. She was not so very ignorant now—ignorant, indeed, beside him—but still knowing something that would make her able to read to him if he liked it, and to understand if he talked of grave things.

She had no fixed thought of what she would be to him when she reached him.

She fancied she would wait on him, and tend him, and make him well, and be caressed by him, and get all gracious pretty things of leaf and blossom about him, and kneel at his feet, and be quite happy if he only touched her now and then with his lips;—her thoughts went no further than that;—her love for him was of that intensity and absorption in which nothing but itself is remembered.

When a creature loves much, even when it is as little and as simple a soul as Bébée, the world and all its people and all its laws and ways are as naught. They cease to exist; they are as though they had never been.

Whoever recollects an outside world may play with passion, or may idle with sentiment, but does not love.

She did not hear what the villagers said to her. She did not see the streets of the towns as she passed them. She kept herself clean always, and broke fast now and then by sheer instinct of habit, nothing more. She had no perception what she did, except of walking—walking—walking always, and seeing the white road go by like pale ribbons unrolled.

She got a dreamy, intense, sleepless light in her blue eyes that frightened some of those she passed. They thought she had been fever-stricken, and was not in her senses.

So she went across the dreary lowlands, wearing out her little sabots, but not wearing out her patience and her courage.

She was very dusty and jaded. Her woolen skirt was stained with weather and torn with briers. But she had managed always to wash her cap white in brook-water, and she had managed always to keep her pretty bright curls soft and silken—for he had liked them so much, and he would soon draw them through his hand again. So she told herself a thousand times to give her strength when the mist would come over her sight, and the earth would seem to tremble as she went. On the fifteenth day from the night when she had left her hut by the swans' water, Bébée saw Paris.

Shining away in the sun; white and gold; among woods and gardens she saw Paris.

She was so tired—oh, so tired—but she could not rest now. There were bells ringing always in her ears, and a heavy pain always in her head. But what of that?—she was so near to him.

"Are you ill, you little thing?" a woman asked her who was gathering early cherries in the outskirts of the great city.

Bébée looked at her and smiled: "I do not know —I am happy."

And she went onward.

It was evening. The sun had set. She had not eaten for twenty-four hours. But she could not pause for anything now. She crossed the gleaming river, and she heard the cathedral chimes. Paris in all its glory was about her, but she took no more note of it than a pigeon that flies through it intent on reaching home.

No one looked at or stopped her; a little dusty peasant with a bundle on a stick over her shoulder.

The click-clack of her wooden shoes on the hot pavements made none look up; little rustics came up every day like this to make their fortunes in Paris. Some grew into golden painted silken flowers, the convolvuli of their brief summer days; and some drifted into the Seine water, rusted, wind-tossed, fallen leaves, that were wanted of no man. Anyhow it was so common to see them, pretty but homely things, with their noisy shoes and their little all in a bundle, that no one even looked once at Bébée.

She was not bewildered. As she had gone through her own city, only thinking of the roses in her basket and of old Annémie in her garret, so she went through Paris, only thinking of him for whose sake she had come thither.

Now that she was really in his home she was happy; happy though her head ached with that dull odd pain, and all the sunny glare went round and round like a great gilded humming-top, such as the babies clapped their hands at at the Kermesse.

She was happy; she felt sure now that God would not let him die till she got to him. She was quite glad that he had left her all that long, terrible winter, for she had learned so much and was so much more fitted to be with him.

Weary as she was, and strange as the pain in her head made her feel, she was happy, very happy; a warm flush came on her little pale cheeks as she thought how soon he would kiss them, her whole body thrilled with the old sweet nameless joy that she had sickened for in vain so long.

Though she saw nothing else that was around her, she saw some little knots of moss-roses that a girl was selling on the quay, as she used to sell them in front of the Maison du Roi. She had only two sous left, but she stopped and bought two little rosebuds to take to him. He had used to care for them so much in the summer in Brabant.

The girl who sold them told her the way to the street he lived in; it was not very far off the quay. She seemed to float on air, to have wings like the swallows, to hear beautiful music all around. She felt for her beads, and said aves of praise. God was so good.

It was quite night when she reached the street, and sought the number of his house. She spoke his name softly, and trembling very much with joy, not with any fear, but it seemed to her too sacred a thing ever to utter aloud.

An old man looked out of a den by the door, and told her to go straight up the stairs to the third floor, and then turn to the right. The old man chuckled as he glanced after her, and listened to the wooden shoes pattering wearily up the broad stone steps.

Bébée climbed them—ten, twenty, thirty, forty. "He must be very poor!" she thought, "to live so high," and yet the place was wide and handsome, and had a look of riches. Her heart beat so fast, she felt suffocated; her limbs shook, her eyes had a red blood-like mist floating before them; but she thanked God each step she climbed—a moment, and she would look upon the only face she loved.

"He will be glad;—oh, I am sure he will be glad!" she said to herself, as a fear that had never before come near her touched her for a moment—if he should not care?

But even then, what did it matter? Since he was ill she should be there to watch him night and day; and when he was well again, if he should wish her to go away—one could always die.

"But he will be glad—oh, I know he will be glad!" she said to the rosebuds that she carried to him. "And if God will only let me save his life, what else do I want more?"

His name was written on a door before her. The handle of a bell hung down; she pulled it timidly. The door unclosed; she saw no one, and went through. There were low lights burning. There were heavy scents that were strange to her. There was a fantastic gloom from old armor, and old weapons, and old pictures in the dull rich chambers. The sound of her wooden shoes was lost in the softness and thickness of the carpets.

It was not the home of a poor man. A great terror froze her heart;—if she were not wanted here?

She went quickly through three rooms, seeing no one, and at the end of the third there were folding-doors.

"It is I—Bébée," she said softly, as she pushed

them gently apart; and she held out the two moss-rosebuds.

Then the words died on her lips, and a great horror froze her, still and silent, there.

She saw the dusky room as in a dream. She saw him stretched on the bed, leaning on his elbow, laughing, and playing cards upon the lace coverlet. She saw women with loose shining hair and bare limbs, and rubies and diamonds glimmering red and white. She saw men lying about upon the couch, throwing dice and drinking and laughing one with another.

Beyond all she saw against the pillows of his bed a beautiful brown wicked-looking thing like some velvet snake, who leaned over him as he threw down the painted cards upon the lace, and who had cast about his throat her curved bare arm with the great coils of dead gold all a-glitter on it.

And above it all there were odors of wines and flowers, clouds of smoke, shouts of laughter, music of shrill gay voices.

She stood like a frozen creature and saw—the rosebuds in her hand. Then with a great piercing cry she let the little roses fall, and turned and fled. At the sound he looked up and saw her, and shook his beautiful brown harlot off him with an oath.

But Bébée flew down through the empty chambers and the long stairway as a hare flies from the hounds; her tired feet never paused, her aching limbs never slackened; she ran on and on, and on, into the lighted streets, into the fresh night air; on, and on, and on, straight to the river.

From its brink some man's strength caught and held her. She struggled with it.

"Let me die! let me die!" she shrieked to him, and strained from him to get at the cool gray silent water that waited for her there.

Then she lost all consciousness, and saw the stars no more.

When she came back to any sense of life, the stars were shining still, and the face of Jeannot was bending over her, wet with tears.

He had followed her to Paris when they had missed her first, and had come straight by train to the city, making sure it was thither she had come, and there had sought her many days, watching for her by the house of Flamen.

She shuddered away from him as he held her, and looked at him with blank tearless eyes.

"Do not touch me—take me home."

That was all she ever said to him. She never asked him or told him anything. She never noticed that it was strange that he should have been here upon the river-bank. He let her be, and took her silently in the cool night back by the iron ways to Brabant.

CHAPTER XXVIII.

SHE sat quite still and upright in the wagon, with the dark lands rushing by her. She never spoke at all. She had a look that frightened him upon her face. When he tried to touch her hand, she shivered away from him.

The charcoal-burner, hardy and strong among forest-reared men, cowered like a child in a corner, and covered his eyes and wept.

So the night wore away.

She had no perception of anything that happened to her until she was led through her own little garden in the early day, and her starling cried to her "Bonjour, Bonjour!" Even then she only looked about her in a bewildered way, and never spoke.

Were the sixteen days a dream?

She did not know.

The women whom Jeannot summoned, his mother and sisters, and Mère Krebs, and one or two others, weeping for what had been the hardness of their hearts against her, undressed her, and laid her down on her little bed, and opened the shutters to the radiance of the sun.

She let them do as they liked, only she seemed neither to hear nor speak, and she never spoke.

All that Jeannot could tell was that he had found her in Paris, and had saved her from the river.

The women were sorrowful, and reproached themselves. Perhaps she had done wrong, but they had been harsh, and she was so young.

The two little sabots with the holes worn through the soles touched them; and they blamed themselves for having shut their hearts and their doors against her as they saw the fixed blue eyes, without any light in them, and the pretty mouth closed close against either sob or smile.

After all she was Bébée—the little bright blithe thing that had danced with their children, and sung to their singing, and brought them always the first roses of the year. If she had been led astray, they should have been gentler with her.

So they told themselves and each other.

What had she seen in that terrible Paris to change her like this?—they could not tell. She never spoke.

The cock crowed gayly to the sun. The lamb bleated in the meadow. The bees boomed among the pear-tree blossoms. The gray lavender blew in the open house-door. The green leaves threw shifting shadows on the floor.

All things were just the same as they had been the year before, when she had woke to the joy of being a girl of sixteen.

But Bébée now lay quite still and silent on her

little bed; as quiet as the waxen Gesù that they laid in the manger at the Nativity.

"If she would only speak!" the women and the children wailed, weeping sorely.

But she never spoke; nor did she seem to know any one of them. Not even the starling, as he flew on her pillow and called her.

"Give her rest," they all said; and one by one moved away, being poor folk and hard-working, and unable to lose a whole day.

Mère Krebs stayed with her, and Jeannot sat in the porch where her little spinning-wheel stood, and rocked himself to and fro; in vain agony, powerless.

He had done all he could, and it was of no avail.

Then people who had loved her, hearing, came up the green lanes from the city—the cobbler and the tinman, and the old woman who sold saints' pictures by the Broodhuis. The Varnhart children hung about the garden wicket, frightened and sobbing. Old Jehan beat his knees with his hands, and said only over and over again, "Another dead—another dead!—the red mill and I see them all dead!"

The long golden day drifted away, and the swans swayed to and fro, and the willows grew silver in the sunshine.

Bébée, only, lay quite still and never spoke. The starling sat above her head; his wings drooped, and he was silent too.

Towards sunset Bébée raised herself and called aloud: they ran to her.

"Get me a rosebud—one with the moss round it," she said to them.

They went out into the garden, and brought her one wet with dew.

She kissed it, and laid it in one of her little wooden shoes that stood upon the bed.

"Send them to him," she said wearily; "tell him I walked all the way."

Then her head drooped; then momentary consciousness died out: the old dull lifeless look crept over her face again like the shadow of death.

The starling spread his broad black wings above her head. She lay quite still once more. The women left the rosebud in the wooden shoe, not knowing what she meant.

Night fell. Mère Krebs watched beside her. Jeannot went down to the old church to beseech heaven with all his simple, ignorant, tortured soul. The villagers hovered about, talking in low sad voices, and wondering, and dropping one by one into their homes. They were sorry, very sorry; but what could they do?

It was quite night. The lights were put out in the lane. Jeannot, with Father Francis, prayed before the shrine of the Seven Sorrows. Mère Krebs slumbered in her rush-bottomed chair; she was old and worked hard. The starling was awake.

Bébée rose in her bed, and looked around, as

she had done when she had asked for the moss-rosebud.

A sense of unutterable universal pain ached over all her body.

She did not see her little home, its four white walls, its lattice shining in the moon, its wooden bowls and plates, its oaken shelf and presses, its plain familiar things that once had been so dear :—she did not see them ;—she only saw the brown woman with her arm about his throat.

She sat up in her bed and slipped her feet on to the floor; the pretty little rosy feet that he had used to want to clothe in silken stockings.

Poor little feet! she felt a curious compassion for them ;—they had served her so well, and they were so tired.

She sat up a moment with that curious dull agony, aching everywhere in body and in brain. She kissed the rosebud once more, and laid it gently down in the wooden shoe. She did not see anything that was around her. She felt a great dullness that closed in on her; a great weight that was like iron on her head.

She thought she was in the strange, noisy, cruel city, with the river close to her, and all her dead dreams drifting down it like murdered children, whilst that woman kissed him.

She slipped her feet on to the floor, and rose and stood upright. There was a door open to the moonlight—the door where she had sat spinning and singing in a thousand happy days; the lavender blew; the tall, unbudded green lilies swayed in the wind; she looked at them, and knew none of them.

The night air drifted through her linen dress, and played on her bare arms, and lifted the curls of her hair; the same air that had played with her so many times out of mind when she had been a little tottering thing that measured its height by the red rosebush. But it brought her no sense of where she was.

All she saw was the woman who kissed him.

There was the water beyond; the kindly calm water, all green with the moss and the nests of the ouzels and the boughs of the hazels and willows, where the swans were asleep in the reeds, and the broad lilies spread wide and cool.

But she did not see any memory in it. She thought it was the cruel gray river in the strange white city; and she cried to it; and went out into the old familiar ways, and knew none of them; and ran feebly yet fleetly through the bushes and flowers, looking up once at the stars with a helpless broken blind look, like a thing that is dying.

"He does not want me!" she said to them. "He does not want me!—other women kiss him there!"

Then with a low fluttering sound like a bird's when its wings are shot, and yet it tries to rise, she hovered a moment over the water, and stretched her arms out to it.

"He does not want me!" she murmured; "he

does not want me—and I am so tired. Dear God!"

Then she crept down, as a weary child creeps to its mother, and threw herself forward, and let the green dark waters take her where they had found her amidst the lilies, a little laughing yearling thing.

There she soon lay, quite quiet, with her face turned to the stars, and the starling poised above to watch her as she slept.

She had been only Bébée—the ways of God and man had been too hard for her.

When the messengers of Flamen came that day, they took him back a dead moss-rose and a pair of little wooden shoes worn through with walking.

"One creature loved me once," he says to women who wonder why the wooden shoes are there.

THE END.

LIST OF PUBLICATIONS

OF

J. B. LIPPINCOTT & CO.

PHILADELPHIA.

Will be sent by mail, post paid, on receipt of the price.

The Albert N'Yanza. Great Basin of the Nile, and Explorations of the Nile Sources. By SIR SAMUEL WHITE BAKER, M. A., F. R. G. S., &c. With Maps and numerous Illustrations, from sketches by Mr. Baker. New edition. Crown 8vo. Extra cloth, $3.

"It is one of the most interesting and instructive books of travel ever issued; and this edition, at a reduced price, will bring it within the reach of many who have not before seen it."—*Boston Journal.*

"One of the most fascinating, and certainly not the least important, books of travel published during the century." *Boston Eve. Transcript.*

*The Nile Tributaries of Abyssinia, and the Sword-*Hunters of the Hamran Arabs. By SIR SAMUEL WHITE BAKER, M. A., F. R. G. S., &c. With Maps and numerous Illustrations, from original sketches by the Author. New edition. Crown 8vo. Extra cloth, $2.75.

"We have rarely met with a descriptive work so well conceived and so attractively written as Baker's Abyssinia, and we cordially recommend it to public patronage . . . It is beautifully illustrated."—*N. O Times.*

Eight Years' Wandering in Ceylon. By Sir SAMUEL WHITE BAKER, M. A., F. R. G. S., &c. With Illustrations. 16mo. Extra cloth, $1.50.

"Mr. Baker's description of life in Ceylon, of sport, of the cultivation of the soil, of its birds and beasts and insects and reptiles, of its wild forests and dense jungles, of its palm trees and its betel nuts and intoxicating drugs, will be found very interesting. The book is well written and beautifully printed."—*Balt. Gazette.*

"Notwithstanding the volume abounds with sporting accounts, the natural history of Ceylon is well and carefully described, and the curiosities of the famed island are not neglected. It is a valuable addition to the works on the East Indies."—*Phila. Lutheran Observer.*

The Rifle and the Hound in Ceylon. By Sir SAMUEL WHITE BAKER, M. A., F. R. G. S., &c. With Illustrations. 16mo. Extra cloth, $1.50.

"Certainly no sporting book we have ever read is more alive with spirit and dashing achievements, and we can guarantee that no one interested in such subjects at all can begin to read without finishing it to the last line, or can lay it down without unbounded admiration for the versatile powers of its hero and author."—*The Round Table.*

Cast Up by the Sea. A Book for Boys from Eight Years Old to Eighty. By SIR SAMUEL WHITE BAKER, M. A., F. R. G. S., &c. With eleven Illustrations by Huard. 16mo. Cheap edition, cloth, 65 cts. Fine edition, tinted paper, extra cloth, $1.25.

"Since the days when 'Robinson Crusoe' first gave pleasure to the host of readers, young and old, which has ever since been multiplying, we doubt if any book of that class has presented a claim equally strong to take its place right squarely up to it, and alongside. The boys will all run to get it, and old boys, too, will find themselves growing young again in the boyish admiration which it will elicit even from them."—*Charleston Courier.*

"The boy, of whatever age, who takes up this fascinating book, will scarcely lay it down till finis or daylight appears."—*Columbus Journal.*

Bulwer's Novels. Library Edition. Complete in forty-two volumes. Large type. 12mo. Cloth, $52.50; Library, sheep, $63; half calf, neat, $105; half calf, gilt extra, $115.50. Each novel sold separately, as below, in cloth, at $1.25 per volume.

The Caxtons............2 vols.
My Novel...............4 vols.
What will He do with It?..3 vols.
Devereux...............2 vols.
Last Days of Pompeii....2 vols.
Rienzi.................2 vols.
Leila, Calderon..........1 vol.
The Last of the Barons..2 vols.
Harold.................2 vols.
Pilgrims of the Rhine....1 vol.
Eugene Aram...........2 vols.
Zanoni.................2 vols.
Pelham.................2 vols.
The Disowned..........2 vols.
Paul Clifford............2 vols.
Godolphin..............1 vol.
Ernest Maltravers.......2 vols.
Alice...................2 vols.
Night and Morning......2 vols.
Lucretia................2 vols.
A Strange Story.........2 vols.

"This edition is in every way a desirable one for libraries; the volumes are of convenient size, the type large, the paper of a superior quality, and the binding neat and substantial."—*Philada. Inquirer.*

"Its convenient form makes it desirable for use in traveling, as well as for library purposes. . . . Book-buyers will do well to purchase this edition for their libraries."—*Pittsburg Gazette.*

"Every gentleman who desires to build up a complete library must have this edition of Bulwer."—*Columbus Journal.*

The American Beaver and his Works. By Lewis

H. MORGAN, author of "The League of the Iroquois." Handsomely illustrated with twenty-three full-page Lithographs and numerous Wood-Cuts. One vol. 8vo. Tinted paper. Cloth extra, $5.

"The book may be pronounced an expansive and standard work on the American beaver, and a valuable contribution to science."—*N. Y. Herald.*

"The book is an octavo of three hundred and thirty pages, on very thick paper, handsomely bound and abundantly illustrated with maps and diagrams. It is a complete scientific, practical, historical and descriptive treatise on the subject of which it treats, and will form a standard for those who are seeking knowledge in this department of animal life. . . . By the publication of this book, Messrs. J. B. Lippincott & Co., of Philadelphia, have really done a service to science which we trust will be well rewarded"—***Boston Even. Traveler.***

The Autobiography of Dr. Benjamin Franklin.

The first and only complete edition of Franklin's Memoirs. Printed from the original MS. With Notes and an Introduction. Edited by the HON. JOHN BIGELOW, late Minister of the United States to France. With Portrait from a line Engraving on Steel. Large 12mo. Toned paper. Fine cloth, beveled boards, $2.50.

"The discovery of the original autograph of Benjamin Franklin's characteristic narrative of his own life was one of the fortunate events of Mr. Bigelow's diplomatic career. It has given him the opportunity of producing a volume of rare bibliographical interest, and performing a valuable service to the cause of letters. He has engaged in his task with the enthusiasm of an American scholar, and completed it in a manner highly creditable to his judgment and industry."—*The New York Tribune.*

"Every one who has at heart the honor of the nation, the interests of American literature and the fame of Franklin will thank the author for so requisite a national service, and applaud the manner and method of its fulfillment."—***Boston Even. Transcript***

The Dervishes. History of the Dervishes; or,

Oriental Spiritualism. By JOHN P. BROWN, Interpreter of the American Legation at Constantinople. With twenty-four Illustrations. One vol. crown 8vo. Tinted paper. Cloth, $3.50.

"In this volume are the fruits of long years of study and investigation, with a great deal of personal observation. It treats, in an exhaustive manner, of the belief and principles of the Dervishes. . . . On the whole, this is a thoroughly original work, which cannot fail to become a book of reference."—***The Philada. Press.***

New America. By Wm. Hepworth Dixon. Fourth

edition. Crown 8vo. With Illustrations. Tinted paper. Extra cloth, $2.75.

"In this graphic volume Mr. Dixon sketches American men and women sharply, vigorously and truthfully, under every aspect."—***Dublin University Magazine.***

Dictionary of Daily Wants. A Cyclopædia em- bracing nearly 1200 pages of Sound Information upon all matters of Practical and Domestic Utility, containing 980 Engravings. One handsome 12mo vol. Half Roxburgh, $3.75.

The "Dictionary of Daily Wants" may be said to have done for matters of Practical Utility in Domestic Affairs what the great naturalist Linnæus did for the Science of Botany. It has brought thousands of useful items, scattered in disorder through an unlimited number of channels, into one arrangement and system, by which they may be easily found and applied.

The sale of nearly 100,000 copies of this work affords the best evidence of its intrinsic value.

Dictionary of Useful Knowledge. A Book of Reference upon History, Geography, Science, Statistics, etc., with 570 Engravings. A Companion Work to the "Dictionary of Daily Wants." Two handsome 12mo vols., containing over 1500 pages. Half Roxburgh, $5.

Lippincott's Treasuries of Literary Gems. Min- iature 4to. Choicely printed on the finest toned paper and beautifully bound in extra cloth, gilt and gilt edges. 75 cts. each; as follows:

I. A Treasury of Table Talk. II. Epigrams and Literary Follies. III. A Treasury of Poetic Gems. IV. The Table Talk of Samuel Johnson, LL. D. V. Gleanings from the Comedies of Shakspeare. VI. Beauties of the British Dramatists. The six volumes in neat box, $4.50.

"A charming little series, well edited and printed. More thoroughly readable little books it would be hard to find: there is no padding in them: all is epigram, point, poetry or sound common sense."—*London Publishers' Circular.*

Mizpah. Friends at Prayer. Containing a Prayer or Meditation for each day in the Year. By LAFAYETTE C. LOOMIS. 12mo. Beautifully printed on superfine tinted paper within red lines. Fine cloth, $2. Extra cloth, gilt edges. $2.50.

This work proposes Morning and Evening Scripture Readings, and an Evening Meditation. The Morning Readings embrace the Psalms twice, and the evening, the New Testament entire, during the year. The Meditations are not expositions of the text, but rather devotional reflections—generally upon the Evening Reading—and intended to follow the Scripture and precede prayer.

The Wife's Messengers: A Novel. By Mrs. M. B. HORTON. 12mo. Tinted paper. Extra cloth, $1.75.

"The writer has produced a capital contribution to the cause of domestic truth, and one which will be read with delight in many a household."—*Ohio Statesman.*

"This story is pervaded by a strong religious feeling. The story is well worth reading on its own merits, and some portions of it are written with a real power that cannot fail to command attention."—*Philada. Evening Telegraph.*

Our Own Birds of the United States. A Familiar

Natural History of the Birds of the United States. By WILLIAM L. BAILY. Revised and Edited by Edward D. Cope, Member of the Academy of Natural Sciences. With numerous Illustrations. 16mo. Toned paper. Extra cloth, $1.50.

"The text is all the more acceptable to the general reader because the birds are called by their popular names, and not by the scientific titles of the cyclopædias, and we know them at once as old friends and companions. We commend this unpretending little book to the public as possessing an interest wider in its range but similar in kind to that which belongs to Gilbert White's Natural History of Selborne."—*N. Y. Even. Post.*

"The whole book is attractive, supplying much pleasantly-conveyed information for young readers, and embodying an arrangement and system that will often make it a helpful work of reference for older naturalists."—*Philada. Even. Bulletin.*

"To the youthful, 'Our Own Birds' is likely to prove a bountiful source of pleasure, and cannot fail to make them thoroughly acquainted with the birds of the United States. As a science there is none more agreeable to study than ornithology. We therefore feel no hesitation in commending this book to the public. It is neatly printed and bound, and is profusely illustrated."—*New York Herald.*

A Few Friends, and How They Amused Them-

selves. A Tale in Nine Chapters, containing descriptions of Twenty Pastimes and Games, and a Fancy-Dress Party. By M. E. DODGE, author of "Hans Brinker," &c. 12mo. Toned paper. Extra cloth, $1.25.

"This convenient little encyclopædia strikes the proper moment most fitly. The evenings have lengthened, and until they again become short parties will be gathered everywhere and social intercourse will be general. But though it is comparatively easy to assemble those who would be amused, the amusement is sometimes replaced by its opposite, and more resembles a religious meeting than the juicy entertainment intended. The 'Few Friends' describes some twenty pastimes, all more or less intellectual, all provident of mirth, requiring no preparation, and capable of enlisting the largest or passing off with the smallest numbers. The description is conveyed by examples that are themselves 'as good as a play.' The book deserves a wide circulation, as it is the missionary of much social pleasure, and demands no more costly apparatus than ready wit and genial disposition." — *Philada. North American.*

Cameos from English History. By the author of

"The Heir of Redclyffe," &c. With marginal Index. 12mo. Tinted paper. Cloth, $1.25; extra cloth, $1.75.

"History is presented in a very attractive and interesting form for young folks in this work."—*Pittsburg Gazette.*

"An excellent design happily executed." —*N. Y. Times.*

The Diamond Edition of the Poetical Works of

Robert Burns. Edited by REV. R. A. WILLMOTT. New edition. With numerous additions. 18mo. Tinted paper. Fine cloth, $1.

"This small, square, compact volume is printed in clear type, and contains, in three hundred pages, the whole of Burns' poems, with a glossary and index. It is cheap, elegant and convenient, bringing the works of one of the most popular of British poets within the means of every reader."—*Boston Even. Transcript.*

Agnes Wentworth. A Novel. By E. Foxton, author of "Herman," and "Sir Pavcn and St. Pavon." 12mo. Tinted paper. Extra cloth, $1.50.

"This is a very interesting and well-told story. There is a naturalness in the grouping of the characters, and a clearness of definition, which make the story pleasant and fascinating. Phases of life are also presented in terse and vigorous words. . . . It is high-toned and much above the average of most of the novels issuing fiom the press."—*Pittsburg Gazette.*

"A novel which has the merit of being written in graceful and clear style, while it tells an interesting story."—*The Independent.*

Siena. A Poem. By A. C. Swinburne. [Republished from *Lippincott's Magazine.*] With Notes. 16mo. Tinted paper. Paper covers, 25 cts.

"Is polished with great care, and is by far the best composition we can recall from Swinburne's pen, in more than one of its effects."—*Philada. North American.*

"One of the most elaborate as well as the most unexceptionable of his productions."—*N. Y. Evening Post.*

Recollections of Persons and Places in the West. By H. M. BRACKENRIDGE, a native of the West; Traveler, Author Jurist. New edition, enlarged. 12mo. Toned paper. Fine cloth, $2.

"A very pleasant book it is, describing, in an autobiographical form, what was 'The West' of this country half a century ago."—*Philada. Press.*

"The writer of these 'Recollections' was born in 1786, and his book is accordingly full of interesting facts and anecdotes respecting a period of Western history, which, when the rapid growth of the country is considered, may almost be called Pre-Adamite."—*Boston Evening Transcript.*

Infelicia. A Volume of Poems. By Adah Isaacs MENKEN. 16mo. Toned paper. Neat cloth, $1. Paper cover, 75 cts. With Portrait of Author, and Letter of Mr. Charles Dickens, from a Steel Engraving. Fine cloth, beveled boards, gilt top, $1.50.

"Some of the poems are forcible, others are graceful and tender, but all are pervaded by a spirit of sadness."—*Washington Evening Star.*

"The volume is interesting, as revealing a something that lay beyond the vulgar eyes that took the liberty of license with the living author's form, and it serves to drape the unhappy life with the mantle of a proper human charity. For herein are visible the vague reachings after and reminiscences of higher things."—*Cincinnati Evening Chronicle.*

Dallas Galbraith. A Novel. By Mrs. R. HardING DAVIS, author of "Waiting for the Verdict," "Margaret Howth," "Life in the Iron Mills," &c. 8vo. Fine cloth, $2.

"One of the best novels ever written for an American magazine."—*Philada. Morning Post.*

"The story is most happily written in all respects."—*The North American.*

"As a specimen of her wonderful intensity and passionate sympathies, this sustained and wholly noble romance is equal or superior to any previous achievement."—*Philada. Evening Bulletin.*

"We therefore seize the opportunity to say that this is a story of unusual power, opening so as to awaken interest. and maintaining the interest to the end."—*The National Baptist.*

Beatrice. A Poem. By Hon. Roden Noel.

Square 16mo. Tinted paper. Extra cloth, gilt top, $1.

"It is impossible to read the poem through without being powerfully moved. There are passages in it which for intensity and tenderness, clear and vivid vision, spontaneous and delicate sympathy, may be compared with the best efforts of our best living writers."—*London Spectator.*

"Mr. Noel has a fruitful imagination, and such a thorough command of language as to link the heart and tongue in that union from which only true poesy is born."—*N. O. Times.*

"Mr. Noel has no rival. He sings with fairy-like and subtle power."—*London Athenæum*

Breaking a Butterfly; or, Blanche Ellerslie's

Ending. A Novel. By the author of "Guy Livingstone," &c. Author's Edition. With Illustrations. 12mo. Extra cloth, $1.50. Paper cover, 50 cts.

"It is a charming story of English life, and marked by the well-known characterstics of the author's style, in which the gorgeous descriptions of manhood are predominant."—*Buffalo Express.*

"It is intensely interesting, full of life and spirit, and throughout is written in the gifted author's most captivating vein."—*Philada. Age.*

"It is a story which every one will find interesting; and it is written with an easy grace indicative of good taste and large experience."—*Albany Journal.*

The Voice in Singing. From the German of

Emma Seiler. New edition. Revised and enlarged. 12mo. Extra cloth. Ornamented. $1.50.

"We would earnestly advise all interested in any way in the vocal organs to read and thoroughly digest this remarkable work."—*Boston Musical Times.*

"It is meeting with the favor of all our authorities, and is a very valuable work. To any one engaged in teaching cultivation of the voice, or making singing a study, it will prove an efficient assistant."—*Loomis' Musical Journal*

"This remarkable book is of special interest to teachers and scholars of vocal music. It is, however, of value to that much larger number of persons who love music for its own sake. Here, almost for the first time in English, and certainly for the first time in an American book, we have a satisfactory explanation of the physiology and æsthetics of the art divine."—*Philada. North American.*

Abraham Page, Esq. Life and Opinions of

Abraham Page, Esq. 12mo. Tinted paper. Fine cloth, $1.50.

"It is really refreshing, in these days of sensational stuff, to fall upon a book like this, written with the easy, well-bred air of a gentleman, and the grace and culture of a scholar."—*Baltimore Leader.*

What I Know about Ben Eccles. A Novel. By

ABRAHAM PAGE, author of "The Life and Opinions of Abraham Page, Esq." 12mo. Cloth, $1.50.

"Quite a pathetic story, which, without being at all of the kind denominated *sensational*, will enchain the attention to the very close."—*Pittsburg Ev. Journal.*

Advice to a Wife on the Management of her own Health, and on the Treatment of some of the Complaints incidental to Pregnancy, Labor and Suckling; with an Introductory Chapter especially addressed to a Young Wife. By PYE HENRY CHAVASSE, M.D. Eighth edition, revised. 16mo. Neatly bound in cloth. $1.50.

"From this advice any woman may gather some precious ideas as to the care of her health. The manual is very popular in England, where it has passed through eight rapid editions, and we know of no similar work where an equal amount of doctor's lore is given in the style of plain modern conversation."—*Philada. Even. Bulletin.*

"Possesses undoubted value for those to whom it is addressed."—*Chicago Journal.*

Advice to a Mother on the Management of her Children, and on the Treatment on the moment of some of their more pressing Illnesses and Accidents. By PYE HENRY CHAVASSE, M.D. Ninth edition, revised. 16mo. Neatly bound in cloth. $1.50.

"For such, and for those who want to rear children judiciously, but need proper counsel, the present volume is one of the most valuable treatises ever published. The new edition contains many new notes, and has undergone a careful revision by Sir Charles Locock, the first physician-accoucheur to Queen Victoria."—*N. Y Even. Post.*

Counsel to a Mother: Being a Continuation and the Completion of "Advice to a Mother." By PYE HENRY CHAVASSE, M.D., author of "Advice to a Wife," etc. 16mo. Fine cloth. $1.

This invaluable work treats of the following subjects:

PART I.—INFANCY: Preliminary Conversation; Ablution; Navel Rupture; Diet; Wet-Nurse; Vaccination; Exercise; Sleep; The Bladder and Bowels.

PART II.—CHILDHOOD: Ablution; Clothing; Diet; The Nursery; Exercise; Amusement; A Poem on Childhood; Education; Sleep; The Hair of a Child.

PART III.—YOUTH: Ablution; Management of Hair; Whitening the Skin; Clothing; Diet; Air and Exercise; Amusements; Education; Household Work for Girls; Teeth and Gums; Sleep.

"Simple, practical, intelligible."—*Philadelphia Evening Bulletin.*

"It is full of sound, practical common sense."—*The Household.*

"There is a quiet simplicity and attractiveness about the book which will induce any woman, and especially if she be a mother, to read it through at one sitting, and thereafter to retain it always for consultation and advice. We are more than pleased with it."—*St. Louis Times.*

Maternal Management of Infancy. For the use of Parents. By F. H. GETCHELL, M.D. 16mo. Cloth. 75 cents.

"We warmly recommend it for its good sense, clearness and brevity."—*The Phila. Press.*

"This little work is deserving the careful attention of all entrusted with the management of infants."—*The Inquirer.*

Dictionary of Medical and Surgical Knowledge, and Complete Practical Guide in Health and Diseases, for Families. With 140 Engravings. One handsome 12mo vol. of 755 pages. Half Roxburgh, $2.50.

The Editor of this volume has brought the experience of more than *thirty* years of active practice, and over *forty* years of professiona. study, to the task of preparing this work.

GOOD BOOKS FOR YOUNG READERS.

Deep Down. A Tale of the Cornish Mines. By R. M. BALLANTYNE, author of "Fighting the Flames," "Silver Lake," etc. With Illustrations. Globe edition. 12mo. Fine cloth. $1.50.

"'Deep Down' can be recommended as a story of exciting interest, which boys will eagerly read, and which will give some valuable ideas on a subject about which very little is generally known. The book is embellished with a number of very excellent designs."—*Philada. Even. Telegraph.*

Fighting the Flames. A Tale of the Fire Brigade. By R. M. BALLANTYNE, author of "Silver Lake," "The Coral Islands," etc. With Illustrations. Globe edition. 12mo. Fine cloth. $1.50.

"An interesting and spirited little work."—*Philada. Even. Telegraph.*

Erling the Bold. A Tale of the Norse Sea-Kings. By R. M. BALLANTYNE, author of "Fighting the Flames," "Deep Down," etc. Globe edition. With Illustrations. 12mo. Extra cloth. $1.50.

"It is a bold and stirring tale of the old Norse rovers who conquered and settled in England at various times between the fifth and eleventh centuries. The narrative is interesting of itself, and it gives an excellent description of the manners and customs of the rugged race who inhabited the North of Europe at the dawn of modern history."—*Philada. Telegraph.*

Silver Lake; or, Lost in the Snow. By R. M. BALLANTYNE, author of "The Wild Man of the West," "Fighting the Flames," etc. With Illustrations. Square 12mo. Tinted paper. Extra cloth. $1.25.

"We heartily recommend the book, and can imagine the pleasure many a young heart will receive on its perusal."—*The Eclectic Review.*

Forty-Four Years of a Hunter's Life. Being Reminiscences of Meshach Browning, a Maryland Hunter. With numerous Illustrations. Globe edition. 12mo. Fine cloth. $1.50.

"It portrays the mode of life of the early settlers, the dangers they encountered, and all the difficulties they had to contend with, and how successfully a strong arm and a courageous heart could overcome them. It is a book which will be read with the greatest avidity by thousands in all sections of the country."—*Balt. American.*

*Moody Mike; or, The Power of Love. A Christ*mas Story. By FRANK SEWALL. Illustrated. 16mo. Extra cloth. $1.

This is a story intended for the young folks. It is published in a manner at once neat and attractive, being well printed and beautifully bound. It is also illustrated with several full-page engravings, which impart to it additional attractions.

GOOD BOOKS FOR YOUNG READERS.

Man Upon the Sea; or, A History of Maritime Adventure, Exploration and Discovery from the Earliest Ages to the Present Time. With numerous Engravings. By FRANK B. GOODRICH, author of "The Court of Napoleon," etc. 8vo. Cloth. $2.25.

"It is a delightful work, brilliant with deeds of valiant enterprise and heroic endurance, and varied by every conceivable incident. We have seldom seen a work more agreeable in style or more fascinating in interest."—*Boston Journal.*

"The book will be warmly welcomed by young people."—*Boston Post.*

Old Deccan Days; or, Hindoo Fairy Legends Current in Southern India. Collected from oral tradition by M. FRERE. With an Introduction and Notes by Sir Bartle Frere. Globe edition. 12mo. Illustrated. Fine cloth. $1.50.

"This little collection of Hindoo Fairy Legends is probably the most interesting book extant on that subject. . . . The stories of this little book are told in a very lively and agreeable style—a style few writers of English possess, but which, when it belongs to a lady, is the best and most attractive in the world."—*N. Y. Times.*

Fuz-Buz and Mother Grabem. The Wonderful Stories of Fuz-Buz the Fly and Mother Grabem the Spider. A Fairy Tale. Handsomely Illustrated. Small 4to. Cloth. $1. Extra cloth, gilt top. $1.25.

"Laughable stories comically illustrated for little folks. The very book to delight little boys and girls. Get it for the holidays."—*Pittsburg Chronicle.*

Casella; or, The Children of the Valleys. By MARTHA FARQUHARSON, author of "Elsie Dinsmore," etc. 16mo. Cloth. $1.50.

"It is rich in all that is strong, generous and true."—*Balt. Episc. Methodist.*

"The story is one of the most interesting in ecclesiastical history."—*The Methodist.*

"A lively and interesting story, based upon the sufferings of the pious Waldenses, and is well written and life-like."—*Boston Christian Era.*

Trees, Plants and Flowers: Where and How they Grow. By WILLIAM L. BAILY, author of "Our Own Birds," etc. With seventy-three Engravings. 16mo. Toned paper. Extra cloth. $1.

"In the compass of less than a hundred and fifty pages Mr. Baily gives us 'a familiar history of the vegetable kingdom,' popularly and interestingly written, well arranged, and containing much valuable information and many interesting facts. He is entitled to great thanks for the work he is doing in aiding the development of a taste for and interest in natural history We should be glad to see this book generally in the hands of the little folks; it is written so clearly and pleasantly that they will take to it readily. But there are many grown folks also who would be glad to know something more of botany than they do, but who have neither time nor inclination for ponderous technical and scientific volumes. To these also we can heartily commend Mr. Baily's book."—*N. Y. Even. Mail.*

VALUABLE BOOKS FOR THE FARM.

The Farmers' and Planters' Encyclopædia of Rural Affairs. Illustrated by numerous Engravings of Animals, Implements and other subjects interesting to the Agriculturist. By CUTHBERT W. JOHNSON, ESQ., F. R. S., etc. Adapted to the United States by GOUVERNEUR EMERSON. A new and revised edition. One vol. royal 8vo. Strongly bound. Price $6.

The Illustrated Horse Doctor: Being an accurate and detailed account of the various Diseases to which the Equine Race are subjected; together with the latest mode of treatment and all the requisite prescriptions, written in plain English. Accompanied by more than 400 Pictorial Representations. By EDWARD MAYHEW, M. R. C. V. S. Tinted paper. 8vo. Cloth. $3.

The Illustrated Horse Management: Containing Descriptive Remarks upon Anatomy, Medicine, Shoeing, Teeth, Food, Vices, Stables; likewise a plain account of the Situation, Nature and Value of the Various Points; together with comments on Grooms, Dealers, Breeders, Breakers and Trainers. Also on Carriages and Harness. Embellished with more than 400 Engravings. By EDWARD MAYHEW, M. R. C. V. S. Tinted paper. 8vo. Cloth. $3.

Sorghum and its Products. An account of recent investigations concerning the Value of Sorghum in Sugar Production; together with a description of a New Method of Making Sugar and Refined Syrup from this Plant. Adapted to common use. By F. L. STEWART. 12mo. Cloth. $1.50.

A Practical Treatise on the Hive and Honey-Bee. By L. L. LANGSTROTH. With an Introduction by REV. ROBERT BAIRD, D. D. Revised and illustrated with 77 Engravings. 12mo. Cloth. $2.

Meehan's Handbook. The American Handbook of Ornamental Trees. By THOMAS MEEHAN, Gardener. 18mo. Cloth. 75 cents.

Youatt on the Horse. Youatt's History, Treat-ment and Diseases of the Horse; with a Treatise on Draught, and copious Index. Liberally Illustrated. 8vo. Cloth. $2.00.

Cottage Piety Exemplified. By the author of "Union to Christ," "Love to God," etc. 16mo. Extra cloth. $1.25.

"A very interesting sketch."—*N. Y. Observer.*

Stories for Sundays, Illustrating the Catechism. By the author of "Little Henry and his Bearer." Revised and edited by A. CLEVELAND COXE, Bishop of Western New York, and author of "Thoughts on the Services," etc. 12mo. Illustrated. Extra cloth. $1.25. Tinted paper. Extra cloth. $1.75. FINE EDITION. Printed within red lines. Extra cloth. Gilt edges. $2.50.

"We are glad to see this charming book in such a handsome dress. This was one of our few Sunday books when we were a school-boy. Sunday books are more plentiful now, but we doubt whether there is any improvement on Mrs. Sherwood's sterling stories for the young."—*Lutheran Observer.*

"The typography is attractive, and the stories illustrated by pictures which render them yet more likely to interest the young people for whose religious improvement they are designed."—*N. Y. Evening Post.*

An Index to the Principal Works in Every Department of Religious Literature. Embracing nearly Seventy Thousand Citations, Alphabetically Arranged under Two Thousand Heads. By HOWARD MALCOM, D. D., LL.D. SECOND EDITION. With Addenda to 1870. 8vo. Extra cloth. $4.

"A work of immense labor, such as no one could prepare who had not the years allotted to the lifetime of man. We know of no work of the kind which can compare with it in value."—*Portland Zion's Advocate.*

"The value of such a book can hardly be overestimated. It is a noble contribution to literature. It meets an urgent need, and long after Dr. Malcom shall have left the world many an earnest pen-worker will thank him, with heartfelt benedictions on his name, for help and service rendered."—*Boston Watchman and Reflector.*

The Geological Evidences of the Antiquity of Man, with Remarks on the Origin of Species by Variation. By SIR CHARLES LYELL, F.R.S., author of "Principles of Geology," etc. Illustrated by wood-cuts. Second American, from the latest London, Edition. 8vo. Extra cloth. $3.

This work treats of one of the most interesting scientific subjects of the day, and will be examined with interest, as well by those who favor its deductions as by those who condemn them.

The Student's Manual of Oriental History. A Manual of the Ancient History of the East, to the Commencement of the Median Wars. By FRANCOIS LENORMANT, Sub-Librarian of the Imperial Institute of France, and E. CHEVALLIER, Member of the Royal Asiatic Society, London. 2 vols. 12mo. Fine cloth. $5.50.

"The best proof of the immense results accomplished in the various departments of philology is to be found in M. Francois Lenormant's admirable *Handbook of Ancient History.*"—*London Athenæum.*

Chambers's Encyclopædia. A Dictionary of Universal Knowledge for the People. Revised Edition. Re-issue of 1870. With Maps, Plates and Engravings. 10 vols. of 832 pages each. Sold only by agents. Illustrated with about Four Thousand Engravings and Forty Maps, together with a Series of from Eighty to One Hundred Elegantly Engraved Plates illustrative of the Subjects of Natural History, now for the *first time* appearing in the work.

PRICE PER VOLUME:

Extra cloth, beveled boards...	$5.50	Half calf, gilt extra, marb. ed.	$7.50
Library sheep, marbled edges.	6.00	Half Russia, red edges...........	8.00
Half Turkey morocco.............	6.50	Turkey antique, gilt edges.....	9.50
Half Turkey Roxb., gilt top...	7.00		

"It is just such a book of reference as every man has occasion for."—*From* WM. C. BRYANT.

"I regard it as an admirable work."—*From* REV. ISAAC FERRIS, *Chancellor of the University of City of New York.*.

"It is indeed just what it proposes to be, a People's Dictionary of Universal Knowledge."—*From* J. BERRIEN LINDSLEY, M.D., D.D., *Chancellor of the University of Nashville.*

"One of the very best and most complete works of the kind ever projected."—*From* HENRY T. TUCKERMAN.

"A treasure house of information."—*From* REV. FRANCIS VINTON, D.D., *Trinity Church, New York City.*

"A model at once of comprehensiveness and condensation."—*From* J. M. P. ATKINSON, D.D., *President of Hampden Sidney College, Va.*

"It is worth more to a family than histories, travels, biographies, etc., of ten times the cost."—*From* REV. ISRAEL ANDREWS, D.D., *Prest. of Marietta College, Ohio.*

"Every public and private library will be richer by the addition of these handsome and instructive volumes."—*From* REV. SAMUEL OSGOOD, D.D., *Pastor of Church of the Messiah, New York City.*

"Upon several topics wherein I have compared the two I find it more full and thorough than the New American Encyclopædia."—*From* REV. JAS. P. THOMPSON, D.D., *Pastor of Tabernacle Church, N. Y.*

"Upon its literary merits, its completeness and accuracy, and the extent and variety of its information, there can be only one opinion."—*From* R. SHELTON MACKENZIE, D.C.L., *Editor of "Noctes Ambrosiæ."*

"In clearness of statement, in the wide range of topics treated, and in the accuracy of research which shows itself on every page, it claims vast superiority over some of its namesakes, which are oftentimes only stale repetitions of each other's blunders."—*From* HON. J. S. BLACK, LL.D., *Late Attorney-General and Secretary of State of the United States.*

"A library in itself."—*From the London Times.*

Morton's and Leeds' Chemistry. The Student's Practical Chemistry. A Text-book for Colleges and Schools on Chemical Physics, including Heat, Light and Electricity, and on Inorganic and Organic Chemistry. By HENRY MORTON, A. M., and ALBERT H. LEEDS, A. M. Illustrated with over 150 Woodcuts. 12mo. Cloth. $2.

In this work the student is furnished with simple and clear explanations of the subjects, and those more advanced in scientific learning with convenient memoranda of important facts, numbers, references, etc. The effort has also been made to embody all the valuable novelties in the branches discussed (many of which have not been introduced in any text-book), and thus bring this work down to the present time.

Wickersham's School Economy. A Treatise on the Preparation, Organization, Employments, Government and Authorities of Schools. By J. P. WICKERSHAM, A. M., *Pennsylvania State Supt. of Common Schools.* Second edition. 12mo. Cloth. $1.50.

SUMMARY OF CONTENTS.

CHAPTER I.—THE PREPARATION FOR THE SCHOOL: I. School Sites.—Convenience of Access—Suitability of Grounds and Surroundings—Healthfulness of the Neighborhood—Beauty of Location; II. School Grounds.—The Arrangements of School Grounds—The Advantages of School Grounds; III. The Plans of Graded Schools.—The Objects of Graded Schools; IV. School Studies.—Studies for Primary Schools, Grammar Schools, High Schools, Colleges; V. School Houses.—Size—Form—Internal Arrangement—Recitation Rooms—The Cellar—Lighting—Heating—Ventilation; VI. School Furniture.—Desks and Seats—Platform—Blackboards—Miscellaneous Articles; VII. School Apparatus; VIII. School Records.—The Forms of School Records—The Objects of School Records.

CHAPTER II.—THE ORGANIZATION OF THE SCHOOL: I. Temporary Organization.—Seating—Times of Opening and Closing—Hours of Recesses and Intermissions—Leaving Seats and Asking Questions—Whispering—General Deportment—Work; II. Permanent Organization.—Provisions Relating to Study—Provisions Relating to Order.

CHAPTER III.—THE EMPLOYMENTS OF THE SCHOOL: I. Study.—The Objects of Study—The Incentives to Study—Proper Incentives to Study—Incentives of Doubtful Propriety—Modes of Study—Characteristics of the Student; II. Recitation.—Objects of the Recitation—Requisites of the Recitation—Methods of Conducting the Recitation; III. Exercise.—Unregulated Exercise—Regulated Exercise.

CHAPTER IV.—GOVERNMENT OF THE SCHOOL: I. School Ethics.—The Classification of Persons engaged in the School—The Duties of Pupils—The Offences of Pupils; II. School Retributions.—Rewards for Good Conduct—Punishments for Bad Conduct; III. School Legislation.—Means of Preventing Disorder—Means of Correcting Disorder—Means of Inducing Pupils to Discharge their Duties of their own Accord; IV. School Administration.—The Detection of Offenders—The Selection of Punishment for Offenders—The Manner of Inflicting Punishment upon Offenders.

CHAPTER V.—THE AUTHORITIES OF THE SCHOOL: I. The Teacher.—The Teacher's Motive—The Teacher's Qualifications—The Teacher's Duties to his Pupils—A Teacher's Life; II. The General School Officers.—Superintendents—School Trustees—School Directors—School Committees; III. The People in Respect to Schools.—Of the Relations of Education in Society—Of the Agencies by which an Education can be obtained.

Hawes's Manual of United States Surveying. A System of Rectangular Surveying employed in subdividing the Public Lands of the United States, etc. Illustrated with forms, diagrams and maps. Constituting a complete Text-Book of Government Surveying. By J. H. HAWES, *Late Principal Clerk of Surveys in the General Land Office.* Crown 8vo. Extra cloth. $3.

"This book embodies in a complete form all the varied information so often sought after by county surveyors and others in regard to the system in use by the United States for surveyings, subdividing sections, running and making boundaries, etc."—*From the New Orleans Times.*

"This volume contains the system of rectangular surveying employed in subdividing sections and restoring lost corners of the public lands. The volume is compact and handsome, and will be found to answer its purpose admirably." *From the Chicago Tribune.*

Wickersham's Methods of Instruction; or, That Part of the Philosophy of Education which Treats of the Nature of the Several Branches of Knowledge and the Method of Teaching them. By J. P. WICKERSHAM, A. M., *Pennsylvania State Superintendent of Common Schools.* 12mo. Cloth. $1.75.

SUMMARY OF CONTENTS.

INTRODUCTION.—TEACHERS REQUIRE SPECIAL PREPARATION—CONDITIONING PRINCIPLES: I. Principles inferable from the Nature of Mind; II. Principles Inferable from the Nature of Knowledge. BUILDING THE FOUNDATION; I. Classification of Knowledge; II. The Genesis of Knowledge; III. The Order of Study.

CHAPTER I.—INSTRUCTION IN THE ELEMENTS OF KNOWLEDGE: I. Informal Instruction in the Elements of Knowledge; II. Formal Instruction in the Elements of Knowledge.

CHAPTER II.—INSTRUCTION IN LANGUAGE: I. Instruction in our Mother Tongue—The Alphabet, Pronunciation, Orthography, Reading, Lexicology, Grammar, Rhetoric, Philology, Composition; II. Instruction in the Dead Languages; III. Instruction in Living Foreign Languages.

CHAPTER III.—INSTRUCTION IN THE FORMAL SCIENCES: I. The Formal Sciences in General; II. Mathematics, Arithmetic, Algebra, Geometry; III. Logic.

CHAPTER IV.—INSTRUCTION IN THE EMPIRICAL SCIENCES: I. The Empirical Sciences in General; II. Geography.

CHAPTER V.—INSTRUCTION IN THE RATIONAL SCIENCES.

CHAPTER VI.—INSTRUCTION IN THE HISTORICAL SCIENCES: I. Methods of Teaching the Facts of History; II. Methods of Teaching the Philosophy of History.

CHAPTER VII.—INSTRUCTION IN THE ARTS: I. Writing; II. Drawing; III Vocal Music; IV. The Arts in General.

Progress of Philosophy. By Samuel Tyler, LL.D. In the Past and in the Future. Second edition, enlarged. 12mo. Cloth. $1.75.

Donald's Etymological Dictionary. Containing the Etymology, Pronunciation and Meaning of every English Word. By JAMES DONALD, F. R. G. S. 12mo. Cloth. $2.50. Roan. $2.75.

This work will, it is believed, supply the want so long felt for a Dictionary based on the etymological relations of words, and exhibiting the results of the latest philological research, at a price quite within the reach of every school."

Leverett's Juvenal. By E. P. Leverett. With Notes. 12mo. Half roan. $1.25.

*Butler's Analogy of Religion. With an Intro*duction, Notes, Conspectus, and ample Index. By HOWARD MALCOLM, D. D. 12mo. Cloth. $1.25.

Atwater's Elementary Logic. *Designed especially for the use of Teachers and Learners.* 12mo. Cloth. $1.50. By L. H. ATWATER, *Professor of Mental and Moral Philosophy in the College of New Jersey.*

"This Manual shows the hand of a master, and will speedily take its proper place as a valuable contribution to the cause of liberal education."—*From the Congregational Quarterly.*

"I observe in Atwater's excellent Manual of Elementary Logic a disposition to unite the real improvements of the analytic with the established truths of the old logic."—*From* DR. JAMES MCCOSH, *Late Professor of Logic in Queen's College, Belfast, Ireland.*

Dr. Blair's Lectures on Rhetoric. *Abridged,* with Questions. 63 cents.

The want of a system of Rhetoric upon a concise plan has rendered this little volume acceptable to the teaching and reading public. Many who are terrified at the idea of traveling over a ponderous volume in search of information, will yet set out on a short journey in pursuit of science with alacrity and profit.

Samson's Art Criticism. *Comprising a Treatise* on the Principles of Man's Nature as addressed by Art; together with a Historic Survey of the Methods of Art Execution in the Departments of Drawing, Sculpture, Architecture, Painting, Landscape Gardening and the Decorative Arts. Designed as a text-book for schools and colleges, and as a hand-book for amateurs and artists. By G. W. SAMSON, *President of Columbia College.* 8vo. Cloth. $3.50.

ABRIDGED EDITION. 12mo. Cloth. $1.75.

"Art criticism, boiled down into small doses for amateurs and students, is the function of Dr. G. W. Samson, President of Columbia College, Washington."—*Philadelphia Bulletin.*

"This work should be in the possession of every lover of the beautiful, and the abridgment deserves to be introduced into all our high schools, and made a part of common education."—*North American.*

Bible Gems; or, Manual of Scripture Lessons. Specially designed for Public Schools, but equally adapted to Sunday-schools and Families. By R. E. KREMER. Illustrated. 16mo. 314 pp. Cloth. $1.

"The purpose of the book, that of introducing more religious instruction into our public schools, meets my entire approbation, and the book itself seems unexceptionable, both in regard to the matter it contains and the manner in which the subject is presented."—*From* J. P. WICKERSHAM, LL.D., *State Superintendent Public Instruction, Penna.*

"The public-school teachers of this State have long felt and expressed the need of a text-book that would aid them in imparting moral instruction to their pupils. The 'Bible Gems,' prepared by a teacher of great experience, will meet this want exactly. It is as free from sectarianism as the Bible itself, and deserves to be largely circulated."—*From* HENRY HOUCK, ESQ., *Deputy Supt. Common Schools.*

*Greek Testament. With English Notes. In*tended for the upper forms of schools and for pass-men at the universities. By HENRY ALFORD, D. D. Abridged by B. H. ALFORD, M. A. Crown 8vo. Cloth. $4.

*Groves's Greek and English Dictionary. Com*prising all the words in the writings of the most popular Greek authors, with the difficult inflections in them, and in the Septuagint and New Testament. Designed for the use of Schools and the undergraduate course of a college education. By REV. JOHN GROVES. A new edition. Royal 8vo. Sheep. $2.50.

Pickering's Greek and English Lexicon; being a Comprehensive Lexicon of the Greek Language, designed for the use of Colleges and Schools in the United States. By JOHN PICKERING, LL.D. 8vo. Sheep. $6.25.

*Leusden's Greek and Latin Testament. By Jo*HANNA LEUSDEN, *Professor.* Crown 8vo. Half roan. $1.75.

Fenelon, M. De. Les Adventures de Telemaque. D'après l'Edition de M. Chas. Le Brun. 12mo. Half roan. $1.40.

*Leverett's Latin Lexicon. Enlarged and Im*proved edition. Embracing the Classical Distinctions of Words, and the Etymological Index of Freund's Lexicon. By E. P. LEVERETT. 8vo. Sheep. $6.25.

The Latin dictionaries now in common use, whatever may be said of the manner in which they do what they propose to do, are essentially deficient in the plan on which they are executed. This work by no means pretends to make up the defect, but aims chiefly to present the classical student with the results of the investigations of the most eminent lexicographers.

*Bledsoe's Philosophy of Mathematics. With Ref*erence to Geometry and the Infinitesimal Method. By A. T. BLEDSOE, LL.D., *late Professor of Mathematics in the University of Virginia.* 12mo. Cloth. $2.

"The author was professor of mathematics in the University of Virginia. This is an evidence of first-class abilities as a geometer. The object of the book is to shed clearer scientific light on the Infinitesimal Calculus. The volume before us does this."—*Universe, Phila.*

"A new treatise on the calculus, in which the whole philosophy of the higher mathematical branches is followed out from the first appearance of its elements in Greek geometry."—*New Orleans Times.*

*Playfair's Euclid. From the latest London edi*tion. Revised and corrected. By J. PLAYFAIR, F.R.S., L. & E. 12mo. Half roan. $1.75.

Moral Reforms, Suggested in a Pastoral Letter. With remarks on Practical Religion. By RT. REV. A. CLEVELAND COXE, Bishop of Western New York, and author of "Thoughts on the Services, etc. 12mo. Cloth. $1.

"This volume will be universally welcomed as a fuller and freer discussion of some of the more practical subjects of Christian life and duty, touched upon in he Bishop's Lenten Pastoral and that of the House of Bishops. . . .

"The book must have a large circulation, for its style and matter will make any one who begins it read it through."—*Utica Gospel Messenger.*

Heart Breathings; or, The Soul's Desire Ex- pressed in Earnestness. A Series of Prayers, Meditations and Selections for the "Home Circle." By S. P. GODWIN. 18mo. Tinted paper. Fine cloth. 75 cents.

"A truly precious little volume, which will doubtless aid the devotions and cheer the way of many a Christian pilgrim."—*Protestant Churchman.*

True Protestant Ritualism. Being a Review of a book entitled "The Law of Ritualism." By the REV. CHARLES H. HALL, D. D., Rector of the Church of the Epiphany, Washington, D. C. 16mo. Cloth. $1.50.

"Dr. Hall has contributed one of the most comprehensive and comprehensible arguments upon the subject which has yet been written. It is well worth the careful perusal of all who are interested in this vexed question."—*Philada. Even. Bulletin.*

Divisions in the Society of Friends. By Thomas H. SPEAKMAN. 16mo. Fine cloth. 63 cents.

"The essay under notice furnishes in a compact form the reasons for the separation of the Society into different organizations."—*Balt. Gazette.*

Life of Philip Doddridge, D. D. With Notices of some of his Contemporaries, and Specimens of his Style. By D. H. HARSHA, M. A., author of "The Star of Bethlehem," etc. NEW EDITION. 12mo. Tinted paper. Extra cloth. $1.50.

"Doddridge is one of the purest and most elevated characters in English religious literature. An American minister, attracted by its excellence, made it a study, and reproduces it in the narrative here given. The work is fairly well executed, and the result is a valuable piece of Christian biography—a book the reading of which will give present pleasure and permanent spiritual advantage to any one who may be able to appreciate it."—*N. Y. Christian Advocate.*

The Threefold Grace of the Holy Trinity. By JOHN H. EGAR, B. D. 12mo. Toned paper. Extra cloth. $1.50.

"It is, in our opinion, one of the ablest and most original contributions to American scientific theology which have been made in our day, and we shall be disappointed if that is not the judgment of the best judges."—*The Amer. Churchman.*

Who is He? An Appeal to those who Regard with any doubt the name of Jesus. By S. F. SMILEY. 16mo. Cloth. 75 cents.

"We hail this little volume, and rejoice at its publication."—*The Episcopalian.*

"Every Friend, every Christian, and most especially every one who is *not* a Christian, should possess and read it."—*Friends' Review.*

Ecce Deus Homo; or, The Work and Kingdom of the Christ of Scripture. 12mo. Tinted paper. Extra cloth. $1.50.

"There is not a page of the book that is wearisome, tedious or dry. The reader feels that a superior intellect is not here weaving a web around him. Amid such terse, short, pithy sentences the light must shine, and misconception is quite impossible."—*The Episcopalian.*

. . . "It seems to be a clear, concise presentation of substantially the common doctrine of the Church on this subject."—*The Congregationalist.*

"We accept with pleasure, as a good statement of the Christian Church, nearly everything in the volume."—*The National Baptist.*

The Divine Teacher. Being the Recorded Sayings of our Lord Jesus Christ during His Ministry on Earth. Small 12mo. Tinted paper. Neat cloth. $1.25.

"The idea is excellent, the workmanship thoughtful, and the book will be a valuable aid to devotion. The little volume will be highly prized by those who are longing and seeking help that may bring them into closer fellowship with the Divine Master and Lord of the Church."—*British Quarterly Review.*

The Unconscious Truth of the Four Gospels. By W. H. FURNESS, D. D. 12mo. Tinted paper. Extra cloth. $1.25.

"A thoughtful and able work."—*N. Y. Even. Post.*

"A really healthy and refreshing religious book."—*The Liberal Christian.*

"One well worth a close perusal by all who have made the study of the New Testament a specialty."—*Chicago Even. Journal.*

Last Days of our Saviour. The Life of our Lord, from the Supper in Bethany to His Ascension into Heaven, in Chronological Order, and in the Words of the Evangelists. *For Passion Week.* Arranged by CHARLES D. COOPER, Rector of St. Philip's Church, Philadelphia. 16mo. Cloth. $1.

"We have examined this with great satisfaction."—*Boston Christian Witness.*

"The idea is an excellent one, and affords the best possible means of obtaining a correct acquaintance with the Man of Sorrows and the great Immanuel in the most interesting aspect of His life."—*Balt. Episcopal Methodist.*

The Reformation of the Church of England. Its History, Principles and Results. 1514-1547. By REV. JOHN BLUNT, M. A., F. S. A., etc. 8vo. Cloth. $6.

"It is distinctly a learned book. The author is not a secondhand retailer of facts; he is a painstaking, conscientious student, who derives his knowledge from original sources."—*London Times.*

THE

WORKS OF WASHINGTON IRVING.

EDITIONS OF IRVING'S WORKS.

I. The Knickerbocker Edition.—Large 12*mo, on* superfine laid, tinted paper. Profusely Illustrated with Steel Plates and Wood-cuts, elegantly printed from new stereotype plates. Complete in 27 vols. Bound in extra cloth, gilt top. Per vol. $2.50. Half calf, gilt extra. Per vol. $4.

II. The Riverside Edition.—16*mo, on fine white* paper; from new stereotype plates. With Steel Plates. Complete in 26 vols. Green crape cloth, gilt top, beveled edges. Per vol. $1.75. Half calf, gilt extra. Per vol. $3.25.

*III. The People's Edition.—From the same stereo-*type plates as above, but printed on cheaper paper. Complete in 26 vols. 16mo. With Steel Vignette Titles. Neatly bound in cloth. Per vol. $1.25. Half calf neat. Per vol. $2.50.

IV. The Sunnyside Edition.—12*mo, on fine toned* paper. With Steel Plates. Complete in 28 vols. Handsomely bound in dark-green cloth. Per vol. $2.25. Half calf, gilt extra. Per vol. $4.

Embracing the following:

Bracebridge Hall,	Goldsmith,	Granada,
Wolfert's Roost.	Alhambra,	Salmagundi,
Sketch Book,	Columbus, 3 vols.,	Spanish Papers, 2 vols.
Traveler,	Astoria,	Washington, 5 vols.,
Knickerbocker,	Bonneville,	Life and Letters, 4 vols.
Crayon Miscellany,	Mahomet, 2 vols.,	

The reissue of these works in their several forms is unusually elegant. The plates are new, the paper superior, the printing handsome, and each, in proportion to price, combining good taste with economy.

☞ EACH WORK SOLD SEPARATELY. ☜

PRESCOTT'S WORKS.

CROWN OCTAVO EDITION.

COMPLETE IN FIFTEEN UNIFORM VOLUMES.

EACH VOLUME WITH PORTRAIT ON STEEL.

Prescott's History of the Reign of Ferdinand and Isabella the Catholic. Three vols. 8vo.

Prescott's Biographical and Critical Miscellanies. With a finely engraved steel Portrait of the Author. One vol. 8vo.

Prescott's History of the Conquest of Mexico, with a Preliminary View of the Ancient Mexican Civilization, and the Life of the Conqueror, Fernando Cortez. In three vols. 8vo.

Prescott's History of the Reign of Philip the Second, King of Spain. In three vols. 8vo.

Prescott's History of the Conquest of Peru, with a Preliminary View of the Civilization of the Incas. In two vols. 8vo.

Prescott's Robertson's History of the Reign of the Emperor Charles the Fifth. With an account of the Emperor's Life after his Abdication. In three vols. 8vo.

Each work sold separately. Price per vol., cloth, $2.50; half calf, neat, $3.75; half calf, gilt extra, marble edges, $4.25; half Turkey, gilt top, $4.50. Complete sets, printed on tinted paper, handsomely bound in green or claret-colored cloth, gilt top, beveled boards. Price, $40.

CHAMBERS'S BOOK OF DAYS.

The Book of Days: A Miscellany of Popular Antiquities in connection with the Calendar, including Anecdote, Biography and History, Curiosities of Literature, and Oddities of Human Life and Character. In two vols. royal 8vo. Price per set, cloth, $9; sheep, $10; half Turkey, $11. Edited under the supervision of ROBERT CHAMBERS.

This work consists of

I.—Matters connected with the Church Calendar, including the Popular Festivals, Saints' Days, and other Holidays, with illustrations of Christian Antiquities in general.

II.—Phenomena connected with the Seasonal Changes.

III.—Folk-Lore of the United Kingdom: namely, Popular Notions and Observances connected with Times and Seasons.

IV.—Notable Events, Biographies and Anecdotes connected with the Days of the Year.

V.—Articles of Popular Archæology, of an entertaining character tending to illustrate the progress of Civilization, Manners, Literature and Ideas in those kingdoms.

VI.—Curious, Fugitive and Inedited Pieces.

The work is printed in a new, elegant and readable type and illustrated with an abundance of Wood Engravings.

A MAGNIFICENT WORK.

A CRITICAL DICTIONARY OF ENGLISH LITERATURE AND

BRITISH AND AMERICAN AUTHORS,

LIVING AND DECEASED.

From the Earliest Accounts to the Latter Half of the Nineteenth Century. Containing over Forty-six Thousand Articles (Authors), with Forty Indexes of Subjects.

BY S. AUSTIN ALLIBONE.

Complete in Three Volumes, Imperial 8vo. 3140 pages. Price per vol.: Extra Cloth, $7.50; Library Sheep, $8.50; Half Turkey, $9.50.

OPINIONS ON THE MERITS OF THE WORK.

"As the work of a single man it is one of the wonders of literary industry. EVERY MAN WHO EVER OWNED AN ENGLISH BOOK, OR EVER MEANS TO OWN ONE, WILL FIND SOMETHING HERE TO HIS PURPOSE."—*Atlantic Monthly.*

"Far superior to any other work of the kind in our language."—*Lord Macaulay.*

"All things considered, the most remarkable literary work ever executed by one man."—*American Literary Gazette.*

"It may be safely said that it is the most valuable and comprehensive manual of English literature yet compiled."—*New York Evening Post.*

"There seems to be no doubt that the book will be welcomed to innumerable reading beings."—*Thomas Carlyle.*

"As a bibliographical work it is simply priceless."—*New York Independent.*

"We are proud that it is the work of an American. We earnestly recommend every reader, student and teacher, and, we had almost said, every patriotic citizen, to secure a copy of Allibone's Dictionary of Authors."—*Boston Evening Transcript.*

"A monument of unsparing industry, indefatigable research, sound and impartial judgment and critical acumen."—*Washington Irving.*

"These volumes are treasuries of English literature, without which no collection of books in our mother-tongue can be considered in any way satisfactory. They contain what can be possessed in no other way than by the ownership of whole libraries of books."—*Philadelphia Ledger.*

"If the rest of the work is as ably executed as that embraced under the first three letters of the alphabet, it cannot fail to be an important contribution to English literature."—*W. H. Prescott.*

"No dictionary of the authors of any language has ever before been undertaken on so grand a scale. For convenience and trustworthiness this work is probably not surpassed by any similar production in the whole range of modern literature. The author has erected a monument of literary industry of which the country has reason to be proud."—*New York Tribune.*

"In the English names alone Mr. Allibone's Dictionary will be far more complete than any work of the kind published in the country."—*London Daily News.*

Dr. William Smith, who is accorded to be one of the greatest compilers of the present age, has paid to the work of Mr. Allibone this generous tribute: "I have frequently consulted it, and have always found what I wanted. The information is given in that clear style and condensed form which is so important in a dictionary."

"Very important and very valuable."—*Charles Dickens.*

Special Circulars, containing a full description of the work, with specimen pages, will be sent, post-paid, on application.

www.ingramcontent.com/pod-product-compliance
Lightning Source LLC
LaVergne TN
LVHW010552110826
845149LV00003B/635